SPORT RULES!

Excel in Sports and Win at Life

MATT YEAGER

DAWSON MEDIA and the DAWSON MEDIA logo are registered trademarks
of Dawson Media. Absence of ® in connection with marks of Dawson Media or
other parties does not indicate an absence of registration of those marks.
ISBN-13: 978-1-935-65-130-7

Cover Design by Blaise Terranova, Tri-Point Teleproductions, Inc.
Cover Photos by iStock Photography
Interior Design by Paul Annan, Omega Creations, Ltd.

LCCN: 2011926514
Printed in the United States of America

15 14 13 12 11   1 2 3 4 5 6 7 8

Contents

Attitude

Growth and Character

Work Ethic and Discipline

Relationships

Intangibles

Living Out the Sports Rules Principles

Acknowledgments

This has been an remarkable experience to put this project together. There are so many people that have had a significant impact on making this a reality.

Wendy, my bride of over twenty years, you are truly amazing. You have been my biggest cheerleader and biggest source of feedback throughout the last year. Thank you for the sacrifice and investment. I love you!

Ellie, Tabi, Hannah, Lydia, and Josh—all of you created much of the material contained in this book. It's been incredible for me to watch each of you develop and grow throughout all the years of sporting events. I love you guys!

Mom and Dad, thanks for allowing me to spend so much time competing in the multitude of sports venues and for modeling such great character to me as I was growing up.

Barb, your dedication to the content editing process has been second to none. Thanks for investing several months of your life in this. Kathy, you were such a big help in fixing the grammar and providing needed feedback early in the editing process. Thanks so much.

Tim, Joni, and Blaise, you blew me away with the cover design. You guys are awesome!

Paul, great job on the website. I am so thankful for you.

I also want to extend a special thanks to so many of you (coaches, athletes, parents, and community leaders) that took the time to read the manuscript and provide feedback. There are so many of you that did that for me, and it would be almost impossible to list each of you, but please know that you played a significant role. Thank you from the bottom of my heart.

Thanks to everyone at Dawson Media for taking this on and guiding me through the process. I appreciate your stellar efforts!

About the Author

Matt Yeager joined the staff of Athletes In Action in 1994. In 2003, he and his wife, Wendy, began working on college campuses in northwest Ohio (primarily at the University of Toledo). In 2010, the Yeagers created a new sports outreach called True Sport Performance which seeks to bring a holistic approach to sports development. They continue to partner as volunteer staff with Athletes In Action on the college campuses of northwest Ohio.

Matt competed on the collegiate level in soccer while a student at the University of Toledo in the 1980s. Since then, he has coached over fifty teams from preschool through high school varsity (soccer and basketball). Presently, he coaches a girls' varsity soccer team at a Toledo area high school.

In addition to graduating from the University of Toledo with a degree in accounting, he has held the CPA certification since 1991. He has made it a passion to pursue leadership development in his own life by participating in numerous professional development opportunities and reading related books.

Matt and Wendy are the parents of five children: Ellie, Tabi, Hannah, Lydia, and Josh. They have experienced parenting children through the ups and downs of soccer, football, baseball, basketball, gymnastics, track, and cheerleading.

Introduction

As a former collegiate athlete who has coached over fifty teams the past twenty plus years, I have found sports to be a tremendous tool to help develop youth into the people they were designed to be. Sports are a microcosm of life, and the principles learned in the competitive arena can be applied to every important area of life.

While athletics inspire remarkable positive characteristics, they offer the opportunity to develop ugly characteristics and attitudes that are destructive to athletes and coaches. The intensity of competition brings out the very best and the very worst in all of us. Over the years, I have observed those effects in my own life and it has caused a remarkable transformation in the way that I approach athletics.

Today, sports rule the lives of many individuals and families whether they realize it or not. The challenge is to figure out how to keep sports in proper perspective and, in essence, develop rules or principles to maximize the venue of athletics. The choices are not always apparent nor are they always easy. Both discipline and wisdom are required to recognize and respond to the demands of sports.

As a young athlete, great intensity always characterized my approach to competition whether it was a neighborhood pickup game or a division championship. That intensity and drive allowed me the opportunity to compete in college. As a young man, I coached with intensity on the sidelines, imitating the attitudes and actions modeled to me growing up.

I discovered that there were aspects of my coaching that were very dysfunctional. There were times when I would leave after a game or practice feeling embarrassed about how I had acted. The heat of the moment somehow brought out attitudes and actions in me that were disappointing. At times, I would justify my actions by thinking that the target of my behavior (players, referees, etc.) deserved what they received and I was right to have acted that way.

As our kids began to enter the world of organized sports, I discovered that the whole youth sports network had grown exponentially. The incredible array of options available to our family seemed endless. We anxiously jumped on the treadmill of youth sports, constantly running kids to practices and competitions.

While in the midst of this, my eyes were opened to see the place that sports has taken in our society. It has risen to become king in many families. Everything revolves around the sports schedules, which become the highest priorities in life. This cultural shift has caused the escalation in the intensity of youth sports competitions. We have all seen the crazy stories about parents losing control in the heat of the moment at youth sports events.

Over the past two decades, I have learned principles which I believe are necessary to help channel sports toward positive impact and to confront the potential negative impact. The chapters in this book are written to provide short and to-the-point exhortations which can be helpful to athletes, coaches, parents, and community youth leaders.

One of my former players, Bethany Brown, wrote a paper for an eighth grade school project about what she learned from soccer. The entire paper is included in Living Out The Sport Rules Principles, but here is a brief excerpt:

> *My coach told us, "There is more to life than soccer, and there is life beyond soccer." These were two valuable lessons that I needed to learn. He taught us these principles*

by discussing topics, such as personal excellence, that I could not only apply to soccer but to life. We learned powerful words like tenacity, teamwork, focusing, *and* determination. *My coach, Matt Yeager, spewed out new words each week that we would use during practice. Here is a man who could teach life lessons through the amazing sport called soccer. Come to think of it, everything I need to know came from him.*

After any loss, he told us to "nail it and press on," which meant to put it behind us. Then, we went over our mistakes and fixed them. I also learned this concept from how Coach acted after a huge defeat. After receiving second place twice to the same team, he told us how proud he was despite our not coming in first. By not pressuring us to be the very best, I learned a great deal about winning and losing.

The principles that he taught me will last forever and I can't thank him enough for teaching them to me. Coach Matt taught me teamwork and humility, life beyond soccer, and that I may not always win everything that I attempt.

To athletes: May these principles provide a roadmap for you to develop your potential as an athlete and cultivate strong character in your life.

To coaches: May you be challenged to become the best you can be in order to achieve the most success on the field of competition and to have the most positive influence on young people.

To parents: May you be motivated to help provide the best environment for your child's development and steer them from the potential negative impact in the midst of their sports.

To community youth leaders: May you invest the time to understand the needs of young athletes and encourage them in their development into young adults.

Important Note to the Reader

One point of caution as you work through the principles contained in this book: You will find some of them to be in tension with one another. This should not catch you by surprise. Good things can become destructive if carried to a dysfunctional degree. Wisdom is required to balance these tensions and help guide your decision-making.

You will also observe that there are some differences in the application of these principles as the level of competition increases. During the learning stages of youth sports, the primary coaching emphasis should be centered on developing all the athletes on the team yet trying to win as much as possible. As the competitive level moves into the high school varsity and college levels, the primary coaching emphasis is on winning competitions while still developing all the athletes.

At the end of each chapter, you will find questions that will help you apply the content of the chapter. These questions will also provide a distinctive differentiation from other chapters which appear to contain similar content. I highly encourage you to make use of this resource.

Attitude

1

Embrace Your Role

Andrew Clarke, known as Dakota, played tight end on the University of Toledo football team. By the end of his junior year, he was in position to break a number of school receiving records and was the third-rated tight end in the country. Everything was going well and an imminent NFL career was in his future.

Suddenly, everything changed. A week after the season ended, Dakota was attending a meeting in the football team room. As he leaned back in his chair, it broke and he fell to the floor. Everyone in the room laughed, including Dakota, and the meeting continued. However, the next morning Dakota had a shooting pain in his back that prevented him from getting out of bed.

An athlete's impact is more than his or her contribution in competition.

Eight months later, Dakota was still plagued by pain, resulting in a medical red shirt for the next season. A year later, he still had not seen much improvement and was able to participate in only about twenty plays during his final season.

During those last two years of his career, I never heard Dakota complain about his situation. On the sidelines, he was the biggest cheerleader of his teammates. Even though he was no longer a starter, Dakota embraced his role. When he was leader on the field, he performed to the best of his ability. When he was sidelined, Dakota became a leader from the team bench.

Athletes often create expectations of what they think their role should be—whether as a starter or expectations of a particular position. It is my experience that those expectations are seldom reality. One of the hardest lessons for athletes to learn is how to accept their role, yet at the same time, work to improve their skill set so they can increase their impact.

An athlete's impact is more than his or her contribution in competition. While Dakota only lined up for twenty plays over two years, he was the only senior team member to receive a standing ovation from his teammates at the team banquet, which included players who would go on to play in the NFL.

Don't underestimate the value of what you can contribute. Whatever your role is, embrace it and maximize it.

Playbook Perspective

I have learned how to be content with whatever I have. I know how to live on almost nothing or with everything. I have learned the secret of living in every situation.
Philippians 4:11-12

Questions for Reflection and Discussion

Athletes

- Do you become bitter when things don't go the way you want?
- Are you committed to the team more than you are committed to your own individual accomplishments and expectations?
- Do you fully understand and embrace your role on the team?

Coaches

- How well do you communicate with your athletes so that they understand their roles on the team?
- Are you able to help those on your team (who may be disappointed with their roles) engage anyway and become productive members on the team?
- For head coaches: Do your assistant coaches understand and embrace their roles? For assistant coaches: Do you understand and embrace your role as an assistant coach?

Parents

- Do you fuel your child's bitterness when things don't go his or her way or do you help your child to deal with it in a positive way?
- Do you accept your child's role on the team even when you disagree with it?

2

Be a Learner

People who "know it all" don't tend to get better. They are lost in their repetition and routine. I see this more in athletes than in coaches. Coaches seem to understand that they need to get better and look for help from outside sources. Athletes (often the best ones) frequently rely on what got them there and sometimes think they know more than the coach. This attitude has kept thousands and probably millions of athletes from getting anywhere close to their potential.

As I have observed coaches and athletes at the University of Toledo over the years, the desire to keep learning separated the excellent athletes from the good athletes. Whether a coach or player, this one discipline has the potential to differentiate the average from the exceptional.

They listen to others who are both more experienced and less experienced.

The people who go out of their way to get better are able to achieve their potential. They read more. They listen to others who are both more experienced and less experienced. They watch others' successes and failures. They ponder their own successes and failures. In short, they seek to learn and soak up whatever information will help them become better athletes or coaches.

The athlete or coach who takes a humble approach as a learner will find nuggets of gold in places where others would not stoop to look. Do yourself a big favor. Set your pride aside and be a learner.

Playbook Perspective

> *Commit yourself to instruction; listen carefully to words of knowledge.*
> Proverbs 23:12

Questions for Reflection and Discussion

Athletes

- Are you a "know it all"?
- Are you coachable?
- Do you seek help to improve from wherever you can find it?

Coaches

- Are you a "know it all"?
- Do you have a mentor?
- To what lengths will you go in order to learn and get better?

Parents

- Do you help your child learn his or her sport?
- Do you seek out other sources to help your child improve in his or her sport?

3

Never, Never, Never Give Up

When I was in third grade, one of my older friends invited me to play baseball with some of his sixth grade friends. I always loved opportunities to compete. Since I had been active playing sports around the neighborhood over the years, I fit in well and held my own.

Over time, I was asked to play other sports with the sixth graders to even out the sides, and I never thought much about the age gap. One time we were playing "Kill-The-Guy-With-The-Ball." Simply put, one guy would have the football and everyone else would try to tackle him. That day I remember getting the ball and eluding everyone, except my friend. Maybe they were afraid of hurting me or were trying to make me feel good. All I remember is the determination and resolve that I had to stay on my feet.

True competitors never give up.

For whatever reason, I have always enjoyed having the odds stacked against me. Often I have been crushed, but sometimes I end up on top. To me, there is nothing more exhilarating than the feeling of overcoming difficult odds.

True competitors never give up. It doesn't matter if the competition is closely contested or if it is a rout. They always find ways to challenge themselves when they are being blown out or when they are well on top in the competition. Their motor continues to work at top speed until the final whistle.

I often tell the teams that I coach to not play according to the score. When a team focuses on the score, their play usually reflects the situation. If the competition is close, they compete harder. If it is not, they tend to relax.

Maximize your effort. Don't play according to the score and never, never, never give up!

Playbook Perspective

The godly may trip seven times, but they will get up again. But one disaster is enough to overthrow the wicked. Proverbs 24:16

Questions for Reflection and Discussion

Athletes

- What situations will cause you to lose your will to compete?
- How do you challenge yourself when the score in a competition is lopsided?
- How can you teach yourself to not compete according to the score?

Coaches

- Does your coaching intensity change when the score is lopsided?
- Do you find ways to challenge your athletes when they are ahead in a lopsided competition?
- How can you model consistency to your athletes regardless of the score?

Parents

- Does your encouragement from the sidelines change when the score is lopsided?
- How are you able to help keep your child's motivation constant?

4

Value Criticism

No matter how old or how experienced I become, I think I will always hate criticism. It just never feels good when someone points out my errors or mistakes. My first knee-jerk reaction is to defend my position.

Over time I've learned not to overreact to those situations or I could miss out on an important lesson. As hard as it seems, I work diligently to actually hear what the person is saying to me. Even if the critique is given with the wrong tone or the wrong attitude, there is often some truth in what they are communicating, providing an important opportunity for me to grow.

Sometimes criticism is easier to take when others choose their words carefully and truly speak with a caring spirit. Other times it is difficult to hold our tongues when we feel like we are being unnecessarily attacked. Yet, it is important to recognize that we can stunt our own growth simply because we do not like

We can stunt our own growth simply because we do not like the tone or attitude associated with the message.

the tone or attitude associated with the message.

Coaches can be rough around the edges when correcting an athlete's performance. However, if the athlete ignores the coach's instruction just because of the way it was delivered, he or she will miss out on the nugget of instruction that could help improve their performance.

There are times when coaches are unfairly criticized. Still, a coach can often glean some helpful elements of truth from those comments or attacks. Often these attacks come when people around the program feel that the team is underachieving.

In order to filter the truth, it can be helpful to ask yourself some difficult questions: How badly do I want to grow and improve? If I am really serious about maximizing my potential, I won't care where the source of my growth comes from (a friend or an enemy). I also won't care about how insulting the information may feel.

When you receive negative feedback about your attitude or performance, it is critical to take a step back and try to view the information from an objective viewpoint. If you can pull your emotions out of the situation, you will be much more likely to benefit from the criticism.

At the end of the day, be careful about reacting too quickly. Put aside your pride. Take a deep breath and listen. Value criticism. You will likely find valuable insights that will serve you well.

Playbook Perspective

Pride leads to conflict; those who take advice are wise.
Proverbs 13:10

Questions for Reflection and Discussion

Athletes
- How do you respond when your performance is criticized?
- Do you look for the kernel of truth when you are criticized?
- Do you despair when you are criticized? If yes, how can you overcome that despair and learn from what was said?

Coaches
- How do you respond when you are criticized or attacked by a parent?
- How have you been able to use criticism to improve your coaching style?

Parents
- How do you respond when a coach criticizes your child?
- How do you help your child respond to it?

5

Be a Team Player

As a boy, I loved football and couldn't wait until I was old enough to put on a helmet and pads. When I was in third grade, I remember going over to the school where football practice was going on. I talked with one of the coaches and learned, to my great disappointment, that I would need to wait a whole year until I could play.

A year passed. I had finally made it to fourth grade so I could play football! In those days, the team consisted of fourth to seventh graders and I was one of the smallest guys on the team. Nevertheless, I worked hard and took my knocks. I don't remember ever playing in a game that year. If I did, it was only for a few plays.

By the time I got to fifth grade, I finally started getting some playing time and my football career was starting to take off. Though I loved the skill positions on offense (quarterback, running back, and receiver), I was put on the offensive line.

I had a role to play even if I wasn't on the field.

Eventually, I was playing center because I was able to long snap to the punter better than anyone else. On defense, I played on the defensive line.

As the next season came around, I became a starter. As a sixth grader, I had the opportunity to play linebacker and finally play a skill position (fullback) on offense. By seventh grade, I became a captain.

One of the most important lessons I learned was that being a part of a team had little to do with playing time during games.

Even though the early years were less glorious than the later years, I realized that my contribution to the team was just as important during my first year as it was in my final year on that football team. I had a role to play even if I wasn't on the field.

In order for a team to climb to its full potential, everyone (athletes, parents, and coaches) needs to place the team development goals above their own personal desires. That can be a very difficult thing to do sometimes, especially when the situation feels unfair.

As a parent watching my kids play sports, I find it is easy to break away from being a team player. My instincts are to evaluate if my child is being treated "fairly" by their coach. Sometimes I have to catch myself in that thought process and determine to see the big picture. As a coach, it is a temptation to focus more on the better athletes' development and to not give as much attention to the weaker athletes.

When individual athletes fully engage to promote the best interests of the team, they discover the joy of fulfilling the role given to them. Every person on the team is important. Even bench players must realize they are the ones making the starters better every day in practice.

Coaches understand that a group of athletes who buy into the team concept will outperform teams who are more talented but play as individuals. So, don't waste your individual talent. Be a team player. You and everyone around you will be better for it.

Playbook Perspective

> *But our bodies have many parts, and God has put each part just where He wants it. How strange a body would be if it only had one part! Yes, there are many parts, but only one body. The eye can never say to the hand, "I don't need you." The head can't say to the feet, "I don't need you." In fact, some parts of the body that seem weakest and least important are actually most necessary.*
> *1 Corinthians 12:18-22*

Questions for Reflection and Discussion

Athletes

- Are you a team player?
- Do you pout when you are not being used like you want to be?
- Do you encourage your teammates even when you are on the sideline?

Coaches

- Does your coaching environment promote team play?
- Do you allow athletes to pout on the sideline?
- Do you develop your inexperienced athletes with the same passion as your top athletes?

Parents

- Do you stir up conflict on your child's team?
- Do you build unity on your child's team? How do you do that?

6

Humility Trumps Pride

"Humpty Dumpty sat on a wall, Humpty Dumpty had a great fall. All the king's horses and all the king's men couldn't put Humpty together again." We are all familiar with that nursery rhyme. Pride is much like Humpty Dumpty. Once it takes root, it is only a matter of time before things in our lives are shattered.

There is a positive aspect to pride. Coaches tell their athletes to "take pride" in their performance or in representing their school. That is a little different because that concept has to do with wanting to perform at the best level possible. However, when I use the word *pride*, in this section, I am talking about arrogance and "tooting your own horn."

We've all watched grandiose professional athletes grandstand after a big score or boast about their athletic prowess in media interviews. Some people may ask, "Is pride acceptable if you can back it up with your performance?" That's a common belief, but it's false! Pride never produces positive results. It is a destructive force that can impact even the best individuals and teams.

It is a destructive force that can impact even the best individuals and teams.

The opposite of pride is humility. Humility brings out the best in an athlete. Athletes and teams who display humility will:

- be coachable (because they look to learn more).
- never underestimate an opponent (because they take each competition seriously).
- play as a team (and individual stats become unimportant).
- not embolden opponents by making foolish statements.

• display sportsmanship whether they win or lose.

Humility does not mean you become someone's doormat, rather that you have a realistic view of yourself and your team. Likewise, you recognize that each competitor is worthy of your respect. Humility does not mean that you lack confidence; rather, it means just the opposite. You understand your strengths and weaknesses. You have confidence in your God-given abilities and work to utilize those strengths for the best results in the competition.

At the end of the day, unchecked pride will become a noose around your neck. If you don't believe me, just watch how many professional athletes have had to eat their words after making brash public statements. For most people, pride is much more subtle. It is an attitude in the heart which will grow quickly causing you to lose your competitive edge.

Always remember that humility outperforms pride every time.

Playbook Perspective

> *Pride leads to disgrace, but with humility comes wisdom.*
> *Proverbs 11:2*

Questions for Reflection and Discussion

Athletes

- Do you have an unrealistic view of your abilities?
- What are your weaknesses?
- Do you appear cocky to others?

Coaches

- When your team doesn't perform at the level you expect, do you ever react poorly because your ego is threatened?
- Are you willing to admit to your team and others when you make a mistake?
- Do you exhibit good sportsmanship during a loss?

Parents

- Does your child's poor performance ever threaten your ego?
- Are you trying to live your dreams through your child?
- Do you exhibit good sportsmanship in a loss to a rival team?

7

Positivity Overcomes Negativity

There is a myth in sports that boisterous negativity, such as screaming threats, berating, or cursing, is the best way to motivate an athlete. At best, it works for the short term. Over the long haul, negativity will beat athletes down and cause many to lose their love and passion for the sport. I have seen this play out at every level from recreational to high-level college competitors. Coaches that remain positive gain the respect and loyalty of their athletes. They also tend to get the best effort from their athletes as well. Teammates who are positive toward each other gain each other's respect and loyalty.

I realize that there will be some who may adamantly disagree with these conclusions and here are some of the reasons.

It is possible to stay positive and still be just as disciplined.

Some coaches believe certain athletes are too soft and need to toughen up. Maybe so, but driving them into the ground will only compound the problem. Another misconception is that discipline will be lost without negative reinforcement. It is possible to stay positive and still be just as disciplined. There needs to be consequences for uninspired effort, lack of concentration, and not following team rules.

Some people believe you can't point out mistakes and still pursue perfection. Not true. Identifying errors can be a positive experience if done with the right tone. Athletes want to improve and get better. Coaches want to improve and get better.

I enjoy coaching and competing much more when I remain positive than when I get stuck in a negative mode. Over the years, I have worked with athletes who have wilted under previous coaches' constant negativity. In time, most of these athletes flourished and some even became all-league performers. All they needed was someone to respect them, believe in them, and, work their tails off to make them better.

I haven't specifically addressed parents yet but the chapter also applies to them. Many parents want so badly for their children to succeed that they become extremely critical, believing that criticism will spur their child to perform better. The main result is family tension and resentment. Parents, always find things to praise in your child's performance.

Like I said before, I always enjoy coaching and competing more when I remain positive—and you will, too. Positivity always trumps negativity.

Playbook Perspective

> *The words of the godly encourage many, but fools are destroyed by their lack of common sense.*
> *Proverbs 10:21*

Questions for Reflection and Discussion

Athletes

- Do you consistently keep a positive attitude during practices and competition?
- How do you help your teammates stay positive?

Coaches

- Have you created a positive atmosphere with your team?
- Are you able to turn negative moments into positive teachable opportunities with your athletes?
- How do you model dealing with adversity to your athletes?

Parents

- Does your child feel affirmed in his/her performance or is he or she always trying to measure up to your expectations?
- How quickly do you change from a positive mood to negative one?

8

Share Your Teammates' Success and Failure

In 2007, I assumed the reigns of a high school girls soccer program. Though my predecessor, who was district coach of the year in his final season, was successful, the number of players committed for the upcoming season had dwindled, causing the future of the program to be in doubt.

Our coaching staff was able to recruit new girls to come out and learn the game. As a result, we had a wide mix of players—some with a lot of experience and some with none. With this in mind, I knew that it was critical for our team to be in the best shape possible because, in most cases, we would be less talented, less experienced, and have fewer substitutes on the bench than our opponents. For us to be successful, we had to be able to outwork them.

Instead, they picked their teammates up and pushed them by running with them to the finish.

A great deal of emphasis was placed on conditioning and stamina. We held out the value of playing hard for eighty minutes, and it required the same effort during practice to accomplish that. The girls responded positively but something happened that I didn't expect.

During one demanding endurance running exercise, the players who finished first went back and started running with the girls who were struggling. One by one as other girls finished, they returned to the exercise to join the slower runners so that the team finished together. It would have been easy for the early finishers to yell at the late finishers to pick it up. Instead, they picked their teammates up and pushed them by running with them to the finish. As a result, that has become a standard procedure for our team.

I can't begin to tell you what that did for the chemistry of the team. They bonded in a deep way. When teammates learn to put aside their selfish ambitions, they are able to maximize their team performance. These girls have received praise from opposing coaches for their tenacity and work ethic even when they have been outmatched. I believe this is largely due to their commitment to each other regardless of their success or failure.

If you want to see what your full team potential can be, get beyond your own world and enter into your teammates' world. You'll discover a new unexpected reality. Share your teammates' success and failure.

Playbook Perspective

Be happy with those who are happy, and weep with those who weep.
Romans 12:15

Questions for Reflection and Discussion

Athletes

• Has a teammate ever "picked you up" when you were struggling?

• Have you ever "picked up" a teammate who was struggling?

• Are you as excited for your teammates when they have success as you are for yourself when you have success?

Coaches

• Do you encourage your athletes to share in each other's joys and struggles?

• Does your team have a strong cohesive bond?

Parents

• Are you as excited for other children's success as you are for your own child?

• Do you encourage your child to share in his or her teammates' successes and failures?

9
Don't Be a Victim

There will be some unfair things that happen during the course of your sports career. If you are a player, it may be a coach that treats you poorly or a teammate that has a goal of making your life miserable. In active competition, it may be an official or an opposing player that tries to single you out to punish you.

If you're a coach, it might be a parent that rides you or simply just continues to create conflict. Still, it could be an athletic director or booster member that doesn't like you and looks for ways to get you removed as coach.

There are usually two reactions that arise in situations like these. One approach is to engage in the conflict and fight back aggressively. The other tactic is to just try to avoid the situation as much as possible while taking a "woe is me" approach. Neither method is generally successful.

A victim mentality will steal your self-concept and rob you of the joy that comes from overcoming adversity.

Aggressively attacking the person making your life difficult never ends well. Your clash with them will ramp up the conflict and become a continuing distraction to the achievement of your athletic goals. While you might feel better about standing up for yourself, you will have caused the conflict to escalate which will work against you in the long run.

Others collapse into being the victim. This person will complain about being treated unfairly to everyone around them in order to gather as much sympathy as possible. Being a victim doesn't make your opposition back off. Taking this approach can actually embolden them and validate their opinion of you.

A victim mentality will steal your self-concept and rob you of the joy that comes from overcoming adversity. The victim doesn't believe that he or she can change or impact difficult circumstances.

However, there is a third approach for dealing with adversity. This is when a competitor assesses what things are within his or her control to change and works hard to make those changes. It might even include humbly going to one's critics and asking for their input or help on how to change the circumstances. Here's a secret: There is something about genuine humility that disarms people and often changes their hearts.

You will find freedom, new strength, and improved relationships when you choose to ignore your natural response. When facing adversity, keep your head up, be humble, and above all don't be a victim.

Playbook Perspective

If you fail under pressure, your strength is too small.
Proverbs 24:10

Questions for Reflection and Discussion

Athletes
- Do you like others to take pity on you?
- Do you blame others for your problems?
- How can you take responsibility for your situation?

Coaches
- Do you take responsibility when your athletes don't understand what you want them to do?
- Do you take responsibility when you don't communicate clearly with athletes and their parents?
- Do you act like a victim when things go sour?

Parents
- Do you blame the coach when things don't go your way?
- Do you teach your child to act like a victim?

Compete Every Day

During my days as an athlete, I always looked forward to playing. Whether it was practice or a game, I couldn't wait to play. Training may have been difficult at times, but I loved the challenge and pushed myself to do everything to the best of my ability.

It didn't matter what sport—basketball, baseball, football, soccer, or swimming—I had the drive to compete. I anticipated the competition every day. What a thrill to put my energies toward being the best that I could be!

As a coach now, I love it when the athletes become motivated and begin to understand the benefits of competing every day. It becomes infectious to others on the team and motivates them to prepare more successfully.

There is more to competing every day than just improving in one's sport.

There is more to competing every day than just improving in one's sport. Something that athletes grasp, but don't always appreciate, is how blessed they are to be able to compete. Often, athletes forget that not everyone has the opportunity or ability to be an athlete.

A competitor should enjoy each opportunity to train or compete just as if it will be their last opportunity. One of the uncertainties in sport is that we don't always know ahead of time when we will be removed from competition. An athlete could be cut or sustain a serious injury. A coach could be fired. In rare cases, an athlete or coach will suddenly pass away.

On two separate occasions during of the fall of 2006, I was called upon to help two different college basketball teams in northwest Ohio deal with the sudden death of their teammate. Those were experiences that are locked indelibly into my memory. Two big, strong young men in good physical condition suddenly had their lives cut short because of undetected heart conditions. I have also worked with scores of other athletes who have seen their athletic careers come to a halt because of injuries. That is why it is so important to treat every day as a gift and make the most of every opportunity.

You never know when your athletic career will be cut short or altered. Competing hard every day allows you to reach your potential. Compete every day! You'll be glad you did.

Playbook Perspective

Good planning and hard work lead to prosperity, but hasty shortcuts lead to poverty.
Proverbs 21:5

Questions for Reflection and Discussion

Athletes
- Are you grateful to be able to practice and compete?
- Do you look forward to the opportunity to practice?
- Do you work hard every day? Why or why not?

Coaches
- Do you expect your athletes to put forth their best effort every day?
- How do you motivate them to compete during practice?
- Do they enjoy competing every day? Why or why not?

Parents
- Do you expect your child to give his or her best effort both at practice and in competitions?
- Are you able to motivate your child so that he or she enjoys competing?

Growth and Character

11

Elevate Your Frustration

Athletics always brought out my deepest passions both as an athlete and as a coach. It didn't matter if it was a pickup game, a huge competition, or a simple game of cards. I have always wanted to win and I always competed with great passion. It is that passion which helped me perform at levels higher than my natural athletic ability should have allowed.

However, passion can have its drawbacks. As a young father, I volunteered to coach my oldest two daughters' soccer team. I looked forward to teaching these young athletes how to play the game. However, as the season progressed, my frustration began to build. Every team we played was more talented and we didn't score a goal the entire season!

I realized that unbridled passion usually has negative consequences.

Toward the end of the season, I began to take my anger and frustration out on the referees and occasionally would throw my clipboard out of disgust. It felt like I just couldn't catch a break for this team. (You may have experienced times like this and can understand those feelings.)

There's more to this story: The team I was coaching was a recreational team for five and six year olds. Most of the kids were playing for the first time. Furthermore, the referees were, in fact, teenagers trying to get experience and make a little money. As my wife, Wendy, sat on the sidelines with the other parents, there were many days she was embarrassed by her husband's behavior.

Thankfully, times have changed and I have grown as a coach. As a varsity coach, I have learned to channel the emotions from frustrating circumstances into positive energy. I realized that un-bridled passion usually has negative consequences. I regularly re-mind myself to stay focused on the competition and not become distracted by things that are unproductive. What does that mean?

If an opposing competitor takes a cheap shot at you, then you have a few choices. The most natural choice is to retaliate and return the favor. This will result in losing your focus on the goal of the competition, which is winning. In essence, you will have allowed your competitor to assume control, rendering you less effective. Another option you have is to back off your level of competition. Again, that gives control of your performance over to your competitor.

My experience tells me that neither of those options is very productive. Rather, we need to channel that anger or frustration toward a heightened resolve in the competition at hand. In other words, you should use that cheap shot as motivation to continue to put forth your best effort.

Frustration can also occur with members of the same team and result in uncontrolled anger. This anger can cause disunity and damaged relationships, both on and off the field. Words spoken in the heat of the moment can have long-lasting consequences and result in broken trust.

A way to help avoid disastrous confrontations between par-ents and coaches, coaches and players, or parents and players, is to ask this question: Are you focusing on respectfully addressing the issue at hand or are you making it personal by attacking a person or their character?

Attacking a person always builds walls that obstruct a relation-ship instead of creating bridges that cultivate relationships. It is critically important to channel your emotional energy into helping that individual deal with the specific problem. You will get more mileage toward the best result and it will require less energy.

Don't succumb to the emotion of the moment. Elevate your frustration.

Playbook Perspective

> *And "don't sin by letting anger control you." Don't let the sun go down while you are still angry.*
> *Ephesians 4:26*

Questions for Reflection and Discussion

Athletes
- Do I allow myself to become frustrated during competition?
- How easily do I lose my focus while I feel frustrated?
- How do I respond to opponents who are taking cheap shots at me?

Coaches
- When the pressure is on and you're becoming frustrated, what do you model to your athletes?
- Have you learned to elevate your frustration so that you are coaching at your best during high-intensity situations?

Parents
- How are you helping your child to overcome frustration when it arises?
- How do you deal with frustration? Have you noticed your child handling frustration in the same manner that you do? If so, have you modeled appropriate frustration-management techniques?

12

Deep inside, every one of us desires to do great things during our lifetime. Often the biggest obstacles to achieving greatness arise from within rather than as the result of outside forces. One obstacle is fear. Unless properly challenged, fear can cripple you and motivate you to make poor choices that you will later regret.

In the competitive environment, fear of failure is a common emotion. Athletes and coaches alike might think, "What if I give my best effort and fail?"

Some of my best achievements as a coach came because something went very wrong.

Rather than remembering that great achievement usually comes after a few experiences with failure, far too many people choose to believe that failure will ruin their lives. The reality is that experiencing and learning from failure is necessary to pave the road to future success.

Some of my best achievements as a coach came because something went very wrong. Those letdowns forced me to innovate and find solutions to improve the team's performance. As much as I disliked the pains of failure, I wouldn't trade those times because of what I gained through them.

I have witnessed certain athletes' performances fall apart at a critical point in the competition because they didn't want to make a mistake. I watched them become paralyzed with fear, therefore, preventing those players from competing at their best.

How do you overcome fear? At the end of the day, your desire to succeed has to be greater than your fear of failure. Players that rise to the top have one thing in common. These athletes are confident that they will make the big play when everything is on the line—and they don't worry about failing. Do they still fail at times? Absolutely! However, the successful athletes don't allow failure (or fear of future failure) to derail them from future success. On the flip side, athletes who allow fear to control them often wind up experiencing the very thing they were afraid would happen.

Have confidence in yourself and enjoy the big moments. Feed your desire to succeed and starve your fear to fail because fear never accomplishes anything.

Playbook Perspective

What I always feared has happened to me. What I dreaded has come true.
Job 3:25

Questions for Reflection and Discussion

Athletes
• Does fear of failure ever keep you from performing at your best?

• What is the worst thing that can happen if you fail?

• What can you do to release yourself from the fear to fail so that you can do your very best?

Coaches
• How does fear of your team underperforming affect the way that you coach?

• Are you afraid of seeing your team underperform?

• Does fear of losing ever change the way you coach?

Parents
• Are you afraid to let your child fail?

• How will you help them overcome failures?

13

Welcome Disappointments

Life doesn't always send us the circumstances that we would choose, but it does send the ones that we need. I discovered the truth of this important life principle in a painful, yet beneficial situation a number of years ago.

I volunteered to coach my daughter's grade school basketball team. The assistant coach (who also had a daughter on the team) was well-meaning, but he didn't know much about the game.

As the season progressed, the assistant coach became increasingly frustrated because I would not play his daughter at point guard. Her skills were not good enough for that role. By the end of the season, however, she matured as a player and I let her play some in that role.

> *I've found that every painful situation and failure have helped me in ways that success never could.*

In addition to the issues with my assistant coach, I also had some parents who couldn't deal with losing often. We lost many games simply because we were the least talented team in the league. Those relational pressures cost me several good nights' sleep that season.

I had to fight the urge to be bitter and angry at the assistant and some of the parents. Instead, it was important for me to learn what I could from this situation. In spite of the perceived unfairness, I was able to look back and reflect on the things that I did as a coach which I could have handled better. As a result, I made some changes in the way that I coach that have made me much better than I was.

I've found that every painful situation and failure has helped me in ways that success never could. Would I choose pain and failure? Absolutely not. However, unwelcome disappointments are my friends.

If we respond well to difficult situations, we can make incredible leaps forward. Welcome disappointment! It can take you to places that you never dreamed you could go.

Playbook Perspective

When troubles come your way, consider it an opportunity for great joy. For you know that when your faith is tested, your endurance has a chance to grow. So let it grow, for when your endurance is fully developed, you will be perfect and complete, needing nothing.
James 1:2-4

Questions for Reflection and Discussion

Athletes

- What have you learned from disappointing situations?
- Are you able to turn setbacks into triumphs?
- Have you been able to help a teammate overcome a disappointment?

Coaches

- What have you been able to learn from discouraging situations?
- How have those circumstances helped you become a better coach?
- How do you help your athletes overcome setbacks?

Parents

- How do you deal with disappointment?
- How do you help your child overcome disappointment?

14

Repetitive Extreme Behavior Gets Ignored

People like to watch colorful sports personalities whether it's an over-animated coach or a superstar athlete. These individuals seem to add spice and flavor to the competition. Their faces portray fierce intensity and it's easy to see how much they care about their sport. However, extreme behavior will lose its intended intensity over time.

Through trial and error, I have learned some important lessons about extreme behavior in sports. I have observed that repeated extremes tend to become commonplace. Coaches that are continually blowing their stack, athletes who try to show up officials when they don't like the call, and parents who nag their kids about poor performance are all examples. There are a limited number of times that a person can exhibit outlandish behavior before others around them come to expect it out of them.

Is there a place for emotion in sports? Absolutely.

As a coach, I know that I have one time or maybe two during a season where I can do something radical to get my players' attention in order to motivate them. For example, it could be having an incredibly, physically demanding practice that leaves them crawling off the field or simply letting the captains run the practice with no input from the coaches. It could also be taking them on a field trip that will help them recognize the opportunities in front of them. I have to choose that spot wisely in order to maximize the team's development.

I have observed athletes of all ages begin to ignore their coach when the coach's shock tactics have been overused. Also, athletes who try to motivate their teammates by regularly using extreme measures (such as guaranteeing wins, going on tirades during practices or games) end up being ignored by their teammates.

Is there a place for emotion in sports? Absolutely. It's a very important element in keeping energy and effort at a high level. If emotion remains positive, it will motivate athletes to high performance. However, when negativity takes over, there is a limited shelf life where it will be helpful.

Repetitive extreme behavior gets ignored, particularly when it's negative. If you want to do something to shake up your team and motivate them, choose your spot wisely!

Playbook Perspective

Some people make cutting remarks, but the words of the wise bring healing.
Proverbs 12:18

Questions for Reflection and Discussion

Athletes

• Have you ever witnessed a teammate, coach, or parent display extreme behavior during a contest? How did it affect you?

• Have you ever been out of control? Describe the situation. What were the consequences?

Coaches

• Does your behavior ever get extreme? If yes, is this a pattern for you?

• How does your behavior in intense situations affect your team relationships?

• Are there better methods you can utilize to motivate your team?

Parents

• Have you ever been the parent that no one wants to sit by at competitions because of your negative behavior? Maybe you haven't noticed or haven't cared.

• What can you do to gain better self-control over your emotions?

15

Toughen Up!

It comes in all shapes and sizes. It also comes from various sources—training, injury, collisions, and disappointments. Pain is just part of competing.

The athletes who are able to find the strength and will to push through when things are hard find tremendous benefit on the other side. It is fairly easy for me to tell how well an athlete will perform in a competition by watching them practice, especially during the grueling training workouts.

One of my challenges as a coach is to help each athlete produce that inner strength which will drive their resolve. There comes a point during difficult training sessions when an athlete hits the wall. The moments that follow will illuminate how tough they really are. The ones with strong internal fortitude will attack the

> *There comes a point during difficult training sessions when an athlete hits the wall.*

workout with a determination that brings new energy. Just the opposite happens with those having weak internal strength.

Here's the good news: Everyone can develop that toughness to overcome pain and difficulty. When athletes that lack confidence begin to understand their capabilities, they push themselves harder to do things that they never thought were possible.

Sometimes the challenges are purely emotional. It might be an extended losing streak or a regular seat on the bench as a backup. Those who have developed mental toughness will become the best they can be regardless of their position on the team and regardless of the team's success.

The difficulty may be overcoming a serious injury so that they can compete again in the future. This requires both mental and physical toughness. Serious injuries usually involve lots of rehabilitation over an extended period of time. Without the proper coaching and parenting support, injuries can suck the life out of an athlete. It is rarely a fun experience, but those who come through it experience a new depth of character.

Obviously, there are times when playing through an injury will make it worse. In those cases being tough just isn't being smart. Most of the time, however, injuries are minor and athletes need to learn to compete through them. This is just part of being an athlete. We are not always feeling 100 percent. In fact, often we are not. Not being at our best should not keep us from giving 100 percent.

Learn to accept pain as part of being an athlete. Toughen up and experience the long-term benefits.

Playbook Perspective

As you know, we consider blessed those who have persevered.
James 5:11 NIV

Questions for Reflection and Discussion

Athletes
- How easily do you give up?
- How well are you able to play through pain?
- What will you do to be tougher and keep fighting when you feel like quitting?

Coaches
- How are you able to motivate your team to play through pain?
- Do you show good judgment to keep an athlete on the sideline when it would be risky to continue competing with an injury?
- Do you ever give up on your team or individual players?

Parents
- How do you help your child overcome adversity?
- Do you ever try to remove your child from a situation so he or she will not have to experience pain? Is this a good idea?

16

Pursue Excellence

As a coach, nothing thrills me more than when I see one of my players staying after practice or coming early so that they can improve. It communicates to me that they actually care about their performance and are willing to pay the price to make themself more valuable to the team.

From morning until dusk, my days were filled with every imaginable sport. Some days, we would have basketball tournaments on our driveway courts. Other days, we would have neighborhood Olympics complete with medal ceremonies.

As I got older and picked up soccer as my main sport, I would spend hours by myself at the school two blocks away working on my foot skills and shooting against the walls of the school building. This seemed normal to me because I was just modeling what I had seen guys a few years older than me do.

Now it seems that normal is just to do the minimum.

Times have changed. Now it seems that normal is just to do the minimum. Show up at practice when the coach schedules it and forget about it until the next practice. I've seen this same attitude in college athletes who have so much untapped potential. They are content to get their scholarship and slide by with the least amount of work.

I've also watched college athletes who were willing to put in the extra work when nobody was watching, and they reaped the benefits. They maximized their athletic ability and knew that they had not taken any shortcuts. These competitors don't spend their time wondering how good they might have been because they did the hard work and can live with the satisfaction of knowing that they maximized their potential.

Does this mean that the sport should consume your life and everything else should be sacrificed? The answer is no. Excellence needs to be pursued in every area of life. Are there times when other areas need to be sacrificed for the sport? Sure. Are there times when the sport needs to be sacrificed for other areas? Absolutely. What we are talking about is pursuing excellence, not fanaticism.

Excellence is working hard and utilizing all the available resources so that I can develop and maximize my potential. Each of us controls how well we will excel in our pursuits. Make sure you don't have regrets. Pursue excellence.

Playbook Perspective

Whatever you do, do well.
Eccelesiastes 9:10a

Questions for Reflection and Discussion

Athletes

- How committed are you to excellence?
- What do you do outside of team practice to get better?
- Do you ever get sloppy when practicing technique or skills?

Coaches

- Do you expect excellence out of your athletes?
- Do you encourage your athletes to spend time on their own getting better (and give them ideas on how to do it)?
- How do you keep them from getting lazy and sloppy during practice?

Parents

- Do you provide an environment that promotes excellence in your child?
- Do you pursue excellence in your pursuits?

17

Entitlement Destroys

The following situations illustrate common problems that athletes, parents, and coaches find themselves in over the course of their involvement in sports. Wendy and I have had to deal with scenarios similar to the ones mentioned in this chapter. As a parent, it is natural to want to protect your child from inequitable circumstances because your child is entitled to fair-minded treatment.

Johnny has joined a youth summer baseball team. This team happens to be pretty good and Johnny is one of the weakest players on the team. The coach is an intense guy and doesn't like to lose. As a result, Johnny shares time with the other weaker

Entitlement sneaks in very subtly.

players on the team. The team wins every game but Johnny becomes frustrated (and so do his parents) because he doesn't feel a part of the team due to his lack of playing time.

Sally is a sixth grade basketball player and has worked really hard to become skilled in her sport. This season her coach is the dad of one of the players on the team. He really doesn't know basketball all that well but thinks he will make things fun for everyone. The coach's lack of basketball knowledge results in poorly planned practices. Unfortunately, the team doesn't improve much. Even worse, the coach believes that his daughter is much better than she actually is, and therefore she gets the majority of playing time while Sally sits on the bench. Sally is hurt and highly disappointed. Her parents are counting the days for the season to be over.

Entitlement means that we behave as if we deserve something that we are not getting. It's not a word that people like to talk about or admit to openly. We can fall prey to this "condition" when we react selfishly to situations when things aren't going our way. However, when we travel down the road of entitlement we destroy an opportunity for ourselves and our kids to develop a new level of character.

I can remember times when I needed to bite my tongue around other parents and avoid being a "cancer." In my opinion, there were certain decisions that created difficult circumstances for my children. However, I refrained from negatively reacting to them. In the end, our family grew into better people because of persevering through the tough times. These challenges have helped our kids develop the character that they will need to have later in life when bigger problems arise.

I think it is more difficult emotionally for parents to take the high road in our present culture because parents are so much more invested in their children's sports than ever before—both financially and in time commitments. Entitlement sneaks in very subtly.

Let me toss out a disclaimer. If there is an abusive, dangerous situation, absolutely take action to address it and find a resolution. But in most cases, an athlete can survive one season and gain important character development.

Think twice before giving into your gut emotions. Consider the long-term benefits of persevering through difficult situations. Remember, entitlement destroys.

Playbook Perspective

Those who control their tongue will have a long life; opening your mouth can ruin everything.
Proverbs 13:3

Questions for Reflection and Discussion

Athletes

- Do you feel that you deserve certain things on your team?
- Do you expect everything to be "fair and even"?
- Do you adjust to situations and make the most of them?

Coaches

- Do you feel like you deserve certain things from your athletes?
- Do you feel like you should be treated a certain way by your athletes' parents?
- How can you adjust your expectations yet still hold athletes and their parents accountable to certain standards?

Parents

- Do you feel that your child is entitled to certain things on his or her team?
- Can those expectations become dysfunctional?

18

Crystal Ball

Expectations are both a blessing and a curse. On the one hand, they can cause us to aspire to great things. On the other hand, unfulfilled expectations can plunge us into frustration and even despair when they are not met.

As an athlete and coach, I have always had this burning desire for perfection. I just can't stand mistakes. I don't think I am unlike any other coach in that regard. When it comes right down to it, I hate being outcoached or seeing my team outperformed. I expect to have the edge over my opponent when I enter into a competition.

I always have a tendency to think that our team is a little better than we really are and that our opponent is not as good as they really are. As a result, I tend to develop expectations of how the competition "should" turn out. When the outcome is different than what I envisioned, I experience a huge letdown.

When the outcome is different than what I envisioned, I experience a huge letdown.

There are some expectations that are unrealistic. For example: I want my players to compete consistently at their best. However, that is an unrealistic expectation. Regardless of the sport, no one turns in identical performances every time out.

We have to remember that every competition is different. Players' energy levels and general health may vary. Officials have different styles, and that can change the flow of the competition. Sometimes there are emotional things happening in the personal lives of athletes and coaches which can greatly affect their performance.

As a coach, I have to keep my expectations in check. When things aren't going well in a game situation, I might want to narrowly focus on things like the team is not playing hard enough or they are mentally disengaging. I have to manage my expectations by remembering to take into account other factors such as the opponent playing very well, game conditions, style of officials, or various personal distractions that might be affecting the players.

While there may not be any scientific evidence to support what I am going to say, I still think that our individual IQs take a big drop in the heat of competition when our emotions take over. We get locked in on only a portion of the factors I just mentioned that are influencing the competition thus causing us to gain an inaccurate picture of what is happening.

The phenomena of mismanaged expectations can also impact athletes and their parents, especially in the junior high and high school years. Students (and their parents) have dreams of scoring a college scholarship just because they have seen good success in their sport. The reality is much different. Only a small group of top-tier athletes receive athletic scholarships at the collegiate level.

Here are a few statistics:[1]

• There are 20–30 million kids playing youth sports. One in four youth stars will become standouts in high school.

• Over one million boys play high school football. Only 41,000 (3.8 %) play in college at a Division I or II schools. Of that number, only 150 players make it to the NFL.

• One million boys and girls play high school basketball. Only 17,000 (1.7%) play in college at a Division I or II school. Only 50 of the 500,000 high school boys make it to the NBA.

[1]http://www.tnsoccer.org/Assets/organized+youth+sports+today.pdf

Failure to manage unrealistic expectations can cause frustration in athletes and their parents, especially when coaches make decisions that appear to negatively impact the athlete's future. The underlying frustration is usually rooted in attitudes of selfishness, pride, ignorance, and entitlement. Ouch! I know that is hard to hear but it is reality.

It is simply human to have expectations. However, you will save yourself tremendous heartache if you take the time to identify any unrealistic expectations and readjust your thinking. Manage your expectations and you will enjoy the ride much more!

Playbook Perspective

What is causing the quarrels and fights among you? Don't they come from the evil desires at war within you?
James 4:1

Questions for Reflection and Discussion

Athletes

• Can you remember a time when unfulfilled expectations left you frustrated? Why did you have that expectation?

• How can you adjust your expectations to be things that are within your control?

Coaches

• What are your expectations for your team? Are they realistic?

• Do you place expectations on your athletes that they are incapable of accomplishing?

Parents

• What are your expectations for your child's sport? Do they need to be adjusted?

• What are your expectations for your child's future? Are they realistic?

19

Sacrifice Wisely

Sacrifice is a concept often discussed in the sports world. Coaches tell their athletes that they need to sacrifice in order to achieve their goals (such as sacrificing time in the summer to shoot 10,000 shots or to come in before school to lift weights). Parents choose to sacrifice in order for their kids to play sports.

However, there is an aspect of sacrifice that I don't hear discussed much: At what point does the sacrifice become excessive? What kinds of sacrifices are we currently making in order to support an athlete's sport? Most importantly, are those sacrifices really worth the cost?

Some families make huge financial sacrifices (which they may not be able to afford) in order for their child to compete in a sport. Some athletes give up opportunities to develop gifts they may have in music or the arts to play sports. Other families give up church attendance, family time, or downtime, in order for their child to compete as expected on weekends.

We need to be cautious about what we sacrifice for the sake of sports.

Sacrifice is looked upon as a good and courageous thing to do, especially if it is for the benefit of someone you love. Common wisdom says that if you care enough about something, you will sacrifice for it. Don't get me wrong. There are noble causes in this world that are worth tremendous sacrifice, but I think we should question how important the role of sports should be.

We need to be cautious about what we sacrifice for the sake of sports. Most student-athletes only play for a limited period of time. We need to evaluate whether more important things (such as family relationships, academics, and faith) are being shoved aside to accommodate the temporary adrenaline rush of sports.

This idea of sacrifice carries a certain amount of tension for me. Like I've mentioned before, I always want to win, and I expect that my teams will work hard. As a coach, I understand that my players and parents have to make sacrifices in order to achieve team goals. However, I try not to make unreasonable demands. I ask myself questions such as: Does it interfere with their academic schedule? Does it disrupt a family holiday? Does it physically put the athlete at risk for serious injury? It is important that I always consider these questions.

Sacrifice is good and beneficial but it can also become a weapon which steals from us things that are more important. Sacrifice wisely.

Playbook Perspective

A prudent person foresees danger and takes precautions. The simpleton goes blindly on and suffers the consequences. Proverbs 22:3

Questions for Reflection and Discussion

Athletes

• What sacrifices are you currently making for your team?

• Are there any additional sacrifices that you need to make in order to help your team?

• Are there sacrifices that you are making for your team that prevent you from investing in other important things or gifts that you have?

Coaches

• Are the sacrifices that you ask from your players reasonable? How would your players and their parents answer that question?

• Are the sacrifices that you are asking for compromising your players' academics or family time?

• How do you balance the needs of the team with the needs of individual athletes?

Parents

• Are you sacrificing important things for the sake of sports? If yes, how will you address this?

• Are there additional sacrifices that you need to encourage your child to make in order to grow as an athlete and help his or her team?

Work Ethic and Discipline

20

Make the Next Play

One of the hardest mental challenges in sports is dealing with mistakes during a competition. Whether you are an athlete or a coach, the striving for perfection drives each competitor to perform error-free. Pitchers want to pitch the "perfect game" with no hits and no runs and quarterbacks want to complete every pass without throwing an interception. Ask any competitive athlete or coach and the primary desire in competition is to perform flawlessly.

Coaches and athletes know that minimizing mistakes on the field of play increase the chance of victory. However, few games are ever really, truly flawless. Mistakes do happen and sometimes, those mistakes have catastrophic results. The danger that befalls athletes in the heat of competition is dwelling on those unfortunate errors. Rather, they must realize that mistakes can serve as good teachers or they can serve to decrease the effectiveness of a competing athlete. The approach makes all the difference in the world.

The danger that befalls athletes in the heat of competition is dwelling on those unfortunate errors.

The next time you are watching a sports event on television, pay attention to what happens after an athlete makes a blunder. Does the coach get in the athlete's face and berate them (as if the athlete didn't know they blew it), or does the coach provide instruction on how to handle that circumstance better in the future? Try to focus on the athlete's face. How does the he react to the mistake? Does the athlete get frustrated and embarrassed, causing future mistakes? Does the athlete focus and improve their mental concentration as the competition continues? Consider how you respond in situations when mistakes are made. Is there a better way for you to handle it?

Mistakes are inevitable but the key is how a person responds to the situation. When former head coach Stan Joplin led the University of Toledo men's basketball program, I had the opportunity to attend a number of their practices. I can still hear Stan encouraging the guys, "Make the next play." Whenever they would make a mistake, I would hear his words, "Pick your head up and make the next play."

Making the next play means:

1. Not dwelling on the past or sulking about the error

2. Maximizing the opportunities in front of you

Can we actually learn from mistakes? Absolutely. Should we try to reduce the errors and push toward perfection? Certainly. More importantly, though, it is imperative that as players and coaches, we always work toward the future and "make the next play."

Playbook Perspective

> *I have not achieved it, but I focus on this one thing: Forgetting the past and looking forward to what lies ahead, I press on to reach the end of the race and receive the heavenly prize for which God, through Jesus Christ, is calling us.*
> *Philippians 3:13-14*

Questions for Reflection and Discussion

Athletes

• Have you made a mistake during a competition that you haven't been able to forget? What happened? How did that mistake change how you saw yourself or how you competed?

• What situations cause you to dwell on past mistakes?

• How has dwelling on those mistakes hurt your performance?

• What will help you remember to put the mistake behind you, learn from it, and make the next play?

Coaches

• How often do you dwell on your athletes' mistakes, causing them to lose focus for the next play?

• Are your athletes timid because they don't want to be yelled at for making a mistake?

• How can you help remind your athletes to play toward the future and not dwell on the past?

Parents

• Is your primary focus on helping your child to achieve his or her potential or on correcting mistakes?

• Can you help your child put a system in place during a competition to remind him or her to make the next play and not dwell on the past?

21

Relentless Dedication
Breeds Success

The fourth grade basketball season had just begun and my daughter, Tabitha, was frustrated because she wasn't getting much playing time on her new team. The previous year, she was one of her team's leaders. Her new circumstances, including a different team and better competition, caught her off guard.

Tabitha and I discussed the situation. She concluded that complaining or getting upset would not change anything. Instead, Tabitha realized that she had to take steps to make herself more valuable to the team. I taught her some ball handling drills, which she regularly practiced over the course of the next couple of months.

Over time her dribbling improved and Tabitha's coach noticed. By the end of the season, Tabitha had earned a starting role. That year was pivotal in her basketball career. She was able to develop into a leader on the court because rather than com-

Skills are built over time, not in an instant.

plaining or quitting, Tabitha chose to work harder to improve her skills. By junior high, she was the starting point guard and held that role into her high school career.

Skills are built over time, not in an instant. A commitment to develop needed skills always pays off in the long run. Some athletes will be motivated and work hard to get better, but many will get tired or bored with the repetition and quit. The individuals that want something badly enough will find a way to keep their commitment to reach their goal.

At the end of each season, I tell my players that their success in the next season will depend on what they are willing to do over the coming eight-nine months. Many of them are along for the ride and will do nothing until the season begins again. Others will take my advice seriously and will make huge leaps in their skills during the off season. They will get into the weight room, work on their ball skills at home, show up in the spring and summer for optional open field scrimmages, and influence others to join them. They are also the ones who, during the season, will stay after practice or come early to work on their skills. Those are the athletes who will be the leaders on the team.

Athletes, keep your commitments to yourself and your long-term goals by being diligent in your development. Remember that relentless dedication breeds success!

Playbook Perspective

> *A hard worker has plenty of food, but a person who chases fantasies ends up in poverty.*
> *Proverbs 28:19*

Questions for Reflection and Discussion

Athletes

- Where do you need to be more consistent in your training?
- Is there anyone who will help keep you accountable?
- Can you visualize the goal of relentless dedication? Describe it.

Coaches

- Are you committed to teaching fundamentals every practice and every competition?
- If you are a youth coach, do you ignore fundamentals when you think it will help you win a competition?
- How can you help motivate your athletes to value relentless dedication?

Parents

- Do you encourage your child to work on his or her skills outside of practice?
- Is it important to you to help maximize your child's development in his or her sport? Why or why not?

22

Study Hard

The more you know about your opponents, the better you are able to understand what it will take to be successful against them. As you understand their strengths and weaknesses, you are able to visualize the techniques and strategies that will allow you to maximize your performance.

I have heard it quoted that most sports are 95 percent mental and 5 percent physical. I'm not sure that I agree with that quote entirely but it certainly makes a great point; the mental aspect of competing is critical to achieving success.

College teams regularly do their homework and scout their opponents thoroughly, especially the ones that are in their conference. I've observed that the athletes who really want to be successful will spend additional time studying the scouting reports and watching more film while the others will do just the minimum required. In fact, one example of this is an NFL player who recently overcame substantial personal issues to return to the NFL. During the season, it has been reported in the media that, since his return to the NFL, he has spent a lot more time in preparation and studying film for upcoming games. As a result, he had his best season and was selected to start in the Pro Bowl.

Take the time to read books and watch instructional videos on your sport.

Athletes who are serious about improving their performance will commit themselves to study. It may not be the most enjoyable activity, but it is one that produces important results.

In addition to studying film and playbooks, athletes can learn from each other. Another aspect of study is watching higher-level athletes compete in their sport. Coaches should encourage their athletes to watch higher-performing playing on a regular basis, whether it is by attending a live sporting event or watching on television. Athletes should observe other players' skills and their intensity. Most importantly, athletes should practice imitating the things that higher-performing athletes do well.

There are a few other learning avenues that coaches and athletes can access and learn from on a regular basis. Take the time to read books and watch instructional videos on your sport. These resources are available at your local library and can actually help you develop these new skills.

Athletes, you will not regret the time spent in research and study. You'll gain an edge in your sport because most athletes will not take the extra time to learn off the field. You will improve in ways that you never imagined. Study hard!

Playbook Perspective

Intelligent people are always ready to learn. Their ears are open for knowledge.
Proverbs 18:15

Questions for Reflection and Discussion

Athletes

• How do you "study" your sport? How is studying for your sport similar or different than studying for a test in class?

• Are there other ways you can study your sport that you are not currently doing?

• Do you study your opponents during competitions? How are you able to capitalize on what you learn during competition?

Coaches

• Do you teach your athletes to be students of the sport?

• Are you continually learning how to better coach your sport? Why or why not?

• How well do you study your opponents?

Parents

• Do you encourage your child to be a student of his or her sport?

• Do you study your child's sport so that you can help him or her develop?

23

Patience Pays Off

It was fifth grade girls' basketball and I was the coach. I discovered quickly that although we had some fairly athletic girls, we were tremendously lacking in skills. In order to develop their skills, I asked each girl to come to every practice fifteen minutes early so we could work on ball handling skills in the hallway before we were able to get into the gym.

As the season unfolded we weren't winning very many games, but I was encouraged by the way our team was progressing. Every team we played usually had two or three players that were better than our best player. We were climbing an uphill battle. The regular season ended with a losing streak extending to thirteen games. As a result, we entered the tournament as the last seed and had to play the top-seeded team in our first game (who was undefeated in the league).

In the opening game of the tournament, we jumped out to a big lead and never looked back. At the end of the game, we had advanced by routing the first-place team. The next night we won again and found ourselves in the championship several days later where we ended up losing a hard fought game.

They persevered by continuing to work on the basics and became a contender.

The team had learned a valuable lesson. Patience pays off. Despite possessing fewer skills at the beginning of the season, the girls improved on their fundamentals and closed the gap with the other teams in their league. They persevered by continuing to work on the basics and became a contender.

Patience is an invaluable character trait in competition. It involves waiting for the right moment to make a move on your opponent so that you maximize your effort.

I preach patience with my high school soccer team day in and day out, especially on defense. A defender who lunges to steal the ball too quickly usually gets beaten and puts their team at risk unnecessarily. Distance runners have to pace themselves and wait for the right opportunity to make their move. Basketball teams wait for the right moment to take the last shot to win the game. Tennis players look for the right opportunity to rush the net and keep their opponent on the defensive.

Patience gives a competitor a strategic advantage. Learn this critical character quality because patience pays off.

Playbook Perspective

> *Enthusiasm without knowledge is no good; haste makes mistakes.*
> *Proverbs 19:2*

Questions for Reflection and Discussion

Athletes

• Are you patient with your development?

• Are you patient during competition or do you get rattled when things don't go well?

• Are you patient in utilizing good timing in order to make the best play or do you impatiently strike too quickly?

Coaches

• Are you patient with your athletes' development or do you become frustrated when they don't get it?

• Do you exhibit patience during competitions?

Parents

• Are you patient with your child's development or do you demand more than he or she can produce?

• Are you able to help your child when he or she is not patient with himself or herself?

24

Don't Cheat Yourself or Your Teammates

As I was searching for a way to better motivate my team during an intense workout, a phrase popped into my head, "Don't cheat yourself or your teammates." It stuck.

Susie played on her school basketball team. When the coach had time during practice to work on individual skills, Susie would take extra breaks when her coach wasn't looking. When she was in the game and her team needed her to make some critical free throws, she couldn't deliver because she didn't take free throw shooting at practice seriously.

There are always certain parts of training that you won't like and may even hate.

There are always certain parts of training that you won't like and may even hate. The temptation during those workouts is to get by with the minimum effort or at least not work at it with your whole heart. These are the days I pull out this motivator—don't cheat yourself or your teammates.

"Don't cheat yourself or your teammates" provides a challenge to maximize personal growth and to recognize that shortcuts will ultimately hurt. It also provides a level of accountability with teammates who don't want someone slacking because it compromises the team's success.

No player wants to think of himself as a cheater or for others to view him as a cheater. I believe that each athlete wants to do his best and experience what it feels like to give his best effort. What most athletes and coaches forget is that most of the time all that it takes is the right perspective and motivation to maximize one's potential.

When the team actually understands the concept, they take ownership of their development and begin pushing themselves individually and corporately toward excellence. Team members encourage those who are struggling and ride those who are slacking. The result will be athletes who demonstrate maturity in their team concept as well as the ability to connect relationally.

Be diligent in the "unpleasant" things and encourage those around you to do the same. Don't cheat yourself or your teammates!

Playbook Perspective

Work hard and become a leader; be lazy and become a slave.
Proverbs 12:24

Questions for Reflection and Discussion

Athletes

• How often do you cheat yourself and your team? Describe how you feel when you see other players on your team slacking off. How do you set your personal standards for working hard during practice?

• What is the cause of your cheating?

• How will you stay focused and maximize your development?

Coaches

• Is your team motivated to not cheat themselves? Why or why not?

• How can you improve their motivation and help them see the benefit of staying focused?

Parents

• Do you ever encourage your child to cheat himself or herself by unnecessarily skipping practice?

• Do you help your child understand that his or her effort directly impacts the team?

Relationships

25

Communicate with Honor and Respect

In the mid-1980s, I was the head coach for a boy's high school varsity soccer team. The team had made good progress and the state tournament arrived. Our first game was hard fought and was scoreless at the end of regulation. After two overtime periods, the score didn't change so we proceeded to a shootout. After the first eight shooters, we were deadlocked at 2–2.

Our player went first and scored. We all waited anxiously as the opposing player lined up for the shot to tie the game. He drilled the shot at the corner but it missed wide. We won and advanced to the next round!

Two days later I received a letter from a parent. Jim had two sons playing on the team. During the course of the game, I had used only twelve players. I had decided that I was going to win or lose that game with our best players on the field regardless of how tired they were. Jim wrote to me because he was disappointed that his older son didn't get in the game and he felt that some of our guys could have used a breather.

I have found that it is very easy to let emotions drive my response to situations.

At first I was a little surprised to receive the letter, but I was impressed at the respect that this father showed me as a young coach. I'm sure that he must have felt a lot of emotion and frustration inside, but he didn't allow that to come out in his communication. As a result, I considered his perspective and it impacted my decision-making in the following game. I did play more players and though we played as well as we could, we lost that game. Twenty-five years later, I am still friends with Jim.

I have found that it is very easy to let emotions drive my response to situations. When I allow my emotions to run unchecked, I make poor decisions in my relationships. As this happens, I question the motives of people that I am frustrated with and easily move into attack mode to "fix" the situation, but usually that makes it worse.

Over time, I have come to realize that approaching frustrating situations with a positive attitude produces much better results. When others are given respect and latitude, they generally give respect back. When I attack a person's character or actions, the natural reaction is for them to become defensive.

However, if I approach someone by sincerely asking them to help me understand the situation and then sharing my perspective, it frees them to take a step back and respond objectively. The environment becomes safe for them and they are able to communicate transparently.

Coaches, parents, and athletes need to respect officials. Parents, athletes, and officials need to respect coaches. Athletes, officials, and coaches need to respect parents. Officials, coaches, and parents need to respect athletes. It may not be easy to do but the long-term benefits are well worth it. Communicate with honor and respect.

Playbook Perspective

> *A gentle answer deflects anger, but harsh words make tempers flare.*
> *Proverbs 15:1*

Questions for Reflection and Discussion

Athletes

- How do you talk about your coach when he or she is not around?
- Do you ever disrespect your coach?
- Do you ever disrespect your parent(s)?

Coaches

- How do you show respect to your athletes? Do circumstances ever change that?
- How do you demonstrate respect to the parents of your athletes?
- Are there ways that you can improve your communication with your athletes and parents?

Parents

- Do you communicate respect to your child's coach even when you are frustrated?
- Do you communicate respect to your child even when he or she performs poorly?

26

I Am Not the Center of the Universe

Jake Barnett came to the University of Toledo on a basketball scholarship in 2009. He was unusually mature and quickly made an impact on everyone around him. He became the first freshman captain in the history of the school and led the team in scoring. He also was six points away from setting the school freshman scoring record.

While all of his basketball accomplishments were impressive, they paled in comparison to his character. He looked for ways to invest in people and didn't get caught up in his press clippings. Whenever there was an opportunity for the university athletes to speak to a group of kids, Jake would be the first to volunteer. Kids would hang on his words and be motivated to pursue their dreams as he shared his life experiences with them.

Whenever there was an opportunity for the university athletes to speak to a group of kids, Jake would be the first to volunteer.

One time he asked me to pick him up at the bus station on a return trip from visiting home. Jake had arrived shortly before I got there and was sitting with his luggage. As I pulled up and stopped, Jake walked over and put his things in the trunk. Before he got in the car, he said to me, "I'll be right back."

I was puzzled by that comment and looked over to see where he was going. Out of the corner of my eye, I saw him approach a guy sitting at the bus stop who looked like he might be homeless. Jake pulled out his wallet and gave him some money followed by a big hug. He walked back and got in the car as if nothing had happened.

Here was a guy who could have lived like he was the center of the universe but chose to live humbly and care deeply about the people he came in contact with. He was always looking to learn and grow from others around him.

Jake's example models the importance of living beyond ourselves. Invest in other people's lives. Value their interests and needs. You will find a deeper satisfaction in life by living outside of yourself. Don't act as if the world revolves around you.

Playbook Perspective

> *Don't be selfish; don't try to impress others. Be humble, thinking of others as better than yourselves. Don't look out only for your own interests, but take an interest in others, too.*
> *Philippians 2:3-4*

Questions for Reflection and Discussion

Athletes
- Do you expect to have special treatment from others?
- Do you put the interests of others ahead of your own?

Coaches
- Are you overly demanding or do you take the needs of others into account when setting practice schedules and other requirements?
- Do you serve your athletes and their parents well?

Parents
- Do you have unrealistic expectations of your child's coach?
- Do you have unrealistic expectations of your child?

27

Don't Demonize Your Opponents

Everyone loves a good rivalry. Ohio State Buckeyes–Michigan Wolverines, New York Yankees–Boston Red Sox, Dallas Cowboys–Washington Redskins. The list goes on and on from professional sports to college sports to high school sports to club sports. It is always the "good guys" (us) versus the "bad guys" (them). We hate for our team to lose to our archrival.

Often these rivalries consist of fun, respect, and long-waited anticipation, but many times the atmosphere becomes ugly. Competitive lines are crossed and the event turns into a war. Well-meaning coaches demonize the opponent in order to raise the emotion and intensity of the athletes heading into competition. Athletes will look for ways to motivate their teammates by stoking the emotional fires of their comrades. What starts out as a fun competition turns into a bitter combat zone.

> **What starts out as a fun competition turns into a bitter combat zone.**

Not too long ago I was coaching my high school girl's varsity soccer team and we were playing one of our rivals. As the game entered the second half, the intensity continued to grow as we had come back from an early 2–0 deficit and claimed the lead 3–2.

The game was physical as both sides were playing hard to win. "No restrictions, no restrictions" the opposing coach yelled in frustration to his players because he was angry that he was not getting the calls that he wanted. He wanted them to do whatever was necessary to win the ball and ultimately the game. I was a little taken aback by his actions, but I had confidence that my team would handle the situation appropriately because they were coached to play hard and not allow their opponents' behavior to keep them from doing the right things on the field.

As the game progressed, one of our girls made a couple of foolish fouls which made the opposing coach irate. The referee appropriately gave her a yellow card on the second foul. A short time later another one of our girls was called for a foul while trying to score near their goal. From my vantage point, it looked like the call could have gone either way so I turned and commented to the girl's parents (who were volunteering at the scorer's table), "That call could have gone either way."

The opposing coach overheard me and immediately started yelling, "How could you say that? Your girls play dirty. I can't believe that you coach your girls to play dirty…" On and on he went. I stood there in disbelief. Here was the guy that earlier was imploring his team, "No restrictions, no restrictions" and now he was accusing me of teaching my girls to be dirty players. He had no idea of the lengths to which our coaching staff went in order to make sure that our players were competing hard but within both the spirit and letter of the laws of the game.

It's extremely easy to think the worst about your opponent. Sometimes opponents are trying to get away with doing the wrong things, but more often than not they are trying to compete as hard as they can in order to win the competition.

When you demonize an opponent, it hurts your competitiveness. It takes your focus off the objective of winning the competition and places it on how you are going to relate to your opponent. It stirs up emotion (most often anger) which decreases your mental edge. If you don't believe me, the next time you see anger or unbridled emotion pop up in a sports event you are watching, objectively observe what happens next. Most of the time the out-of-control athlete will quickly make a mistake or cause a critical penalty that is detrimental to their team.

Your opponent is there to make you better. The harder they compete, the more you are forced to maximize your potential. Value them. Don't demonize them.

Playbook Perspective

Avoiding a fight is a mark of honor; only fools insist on quarreling.
Proverbs 20:3

Questions for Reflection and Discussion

Athletes

- How often do you envision your opponent as the enemy?
- Have you ever tried to injure an opponent?
- How would the competition be different if you showed respect to your opponent?

Coaches

- Have you ever coached your athletes to try to hurt an opponent?
- Do you demonize opponents in order to motivate your athletes?
- Do you give your opponents respect regardless of how they compete?

Parents

- Have you ever had a confrontation with an opposing team's parent?
- Do you ever demonize your child's opponent?
- How do your emotional ties to your child skew the way you view his or her opponents?

28

Respect the Officials

One of the best decisions that I've made was getting my soccer refereeing certification. After years of playing and coaching, I took the classes along with two of my daughters as an activity that we could do together.

The three of us decided to work a tournament together. It was a fascinating experience. I found that what seemed to be an easy job from the sidelines required much mental discipline and quick on-the-spot judgments. Some games were fairly easy and others seemed to have a lot of plays that were difficult to call (no instant replay to help either).

Although I had more experience with the game than almost all of the spectators and coaches, at times I was berated and jeered. Maybe it was a little deserved payback from my earlier years of coaching. It made me realize how foolishly I had acted at times in the past.

One of my daughters found herself in tears when refereeing one game because of the unsportsmanlike intensity displayed by coaches, players, and parents. She shared how it is much more beneficial to have conversations about calls after the game when the emotions are contained

The referee has a different angle than the spectator or coach. Sometimes it's better and sometimes it's worse.

than in the heat of the moment. Though she has enjoyed the opportunity to referee, there have been some painful games that have been discouraging because of uncontrolled behavior.

We all have this desire to see our team win and to see a game officiated "fairly from our point of view." There are things that we fail to realize in our snap judgments about a referee's competency. The referee has a different angle than the spectator or coach. Sometimes it's better and sometimes it's worse. In addition, the referee is focusing on violations of the rules while the spectators and coaches generally focus on the flow and strategy of the game. Last, the referee has no interest in the outcome of the game so the calls should be fairly unbiased.

To be honest, referees do make mistakes and some have very bad days. We have all experienced the frustration that comes when calls don't go our way. Regardless of how well referees do their jobs, they still deserve the respect of athletes, coaches, and fans.

I wonder, though, how many good referees have "retired" because they could no longer stomach the ludicrous behavior of coaches and spectators. Maybe that is part of the reason that the quality of officials is sometimes less than what we would desire.

A few years ago I was coaching a high school soccer game in the state tournament. With ten minutes left, we were holding on to a 2–0 lead. Within minutes, one of the officials called two penalties against us, both of which resulted in penalty kicks that tied the game. Both calls were very questionable and we ended up losing the game 3–2.

Everything inside of me wanted to blast that referee for "stealing" the game from us. The unfortunate turn of events left my team in tears. It was a very difficult moment, yet I managed to bite my tongue and kept my thoughts to myself. It is a decision I have never regretted. I was so proud of our team. While they were devastated, our team was able to congratulate their opponents and wish them well.

Take the high road with officials. Show them respect even if you feel they don't deserve it. You, and those around you, will be better for it.

Playbook Perspective

> *The wise are known for their understanding, and pleasant words are persuasive.*
> *Proverbs 16:21*

Questions for Reflection and Discussion

Athletes

• How do you respond when the official makes a call that you don't agree with or that frustrates you?

• How do you talk about officials on the sideline or after a competition?

• How do you respond to your teammates when they react poorly to an official's decision?

Coaches

• When you disagree with a call, is your communication with the official in a tone of respect or disrespect?

• Do you treat an official differently based on your perception of his or her competence?

• What do you model to your athletes about the respect they should show officials?

• Have you ever been paid to officiate a competition? How might this change your perspective about the difficulty of their job?

Parents

• How do you treat officials when you are attending your child's competition?

• Have you ever seen a competition ruined by parents on the sideline displaying their ignorance and unrestrained intensity? Have you ever done it yourself?

29

Thank Your Supporters

Discipline, patience, and persistence are all important qualities necessary to develop your athletic potential. However, regardless of the level of personal commitment to athletic development, athletes never reach success on their own. There are a variety of "supporting players" committed to helping athletes turn their goals into reality.

For instance, parents (including grandparents and other primary caregivers) play a major role in a student's athletic experience. Whether they are driving their student to practices and games or providing money for additional expenses, parents dedicate a great deal of time and effort on behalf of their

What we become athletically is the sum total of our investment in ourselves plus others' investment in us.

athlete. Additionally, coaches invest many hours, not just in practice, to prepare athletes to perform to the best of their abilities—and most don't get paid much for their work. Even older student-athletes will take an interest in assisting younger athletes increase their performance potential.

What we become athletically is the sum total of our investment in ourselves plus others' investment in us. It is important to remember to thank those who have invested their care, money, and time in us. While these supporting players are not looking for appreciation, parents and coaches are always encouraged when someone takes the time to simply say thank you. As a coach, I am encouraged when one of my players takes the time to say that I made a difference in his or her life. All the practices and hard work to mold that athlete seem like a small investment when I see what the athlete has accomplished.

Take a few minutes out of your schedule to invest in the people who have invested in you. Thank your supporters.

Playbook Perspective

> *Do not withhold good from those who deserve it when it's in your power to help them.*
> *Proverbs 3:27*

Questions for Reflection and Discussion

Athletes

• Have you ever thanked your parent(s) for their help in your athletic endeavors?

• Have you ever thanked your coaches for their time and energy invested in your development?

Coaches

• Have you taken time to appreciate the parents of your athletes?

• Have you thanked those who were instrumental in helping you become the coach you are today?

Parents

• Have you thanked your child's coach for his or her investment in your child's life?

Intangibles

30

It's Just a Game

A few years ago I was with the University of Toledo football team at Central Michigan University. I was on the sideline and happened to be standing near head coach Tom Amstutz at one point during the game. There was a fourth down play on Toledo's own forty yard line. Coach Amstutz glanced over at me with a silly grin and said, "Watch this."

The team was in punt formation but snapped the ball short to a 300 plus pound lineman who proceeded to ramble up the field for twenty yards and a first down. I smiled as I thought about how much fun Coach Amstutz had coaching. To him, it was just a game. Here was a coach who had won conference championships and bowl games but never forgot the purpose of the game.

He lived in the present and made the game fun for his players.

In the midst of the pressures of college athletics, Coach Amstutz enjoyed the moments. He wasn't worried about what the papers would write about him the next day. He didn't have regrets if his gambles didn't pay off. He lived in the present and made the game fun for his players.

While it is important to focus and bring intensity to competition so that your best effort is realized, it is also important to keep competition in perspective. There is a seriousness (life and death approach) that takes place often in the world of sports. The intensity level gets ratcheted so high that it spills into absolutely ridiculous behavior and expectations.

Competition should have an element of enjoyment and fun in the midst of the intense struggle to achieve victory. Studies have shown that roughly three out of four kids quit playing sports by age fourteen mostly because it ceases to be enjoyable.

Most people have experienced or have heard about outrageous conduct from a coach, parent, or athlete at a youth sports event. The level of seriousness and intensity in sports has developed into scary proportions. It's high time to bring sanity and sensibility back into the competitive arena.

It's amazing to watch how outcomes in sports events motivate peoples' behavior. Over the years, we've seen celebrations turn into riots. We've also seen athletes and referees ridiculed (and even murdered) for making a mistake that cost their team a victory in a major competition.

Win or lose, competition needs to be kept in perspective. Take a cue from coach Amstutz and enjoy the moment. Remember, it's just a game.

Playbook Perspective

So I concluded there is nothing better than to be happy and enjoy ourselves as long as we can. And people should eat and drink and enjoy the fruits of their labor, for these are gifts from God.
Ecclesiastes 3:12-13

Questions for Reflection and Discussion

Athletes

- Do you enjoy competing?
- When you lose a competition, does it ruin your day?
- What takes away the joy of competing? What can you do to change this?

Coaches

- Does your intensity level ever take the fun out of competition?
- Does losing ruin your day?
- Can you have more fun coaching without sacrificing intensity and focus?

Parents

- Do you enjoy watching your child compete or do you get caught up in the score?
- How can you help your child enjoy the sport more?

31

Trust Those Around You

Although this may be obvious to most people, trust is one of the most important characteristics of a successful athlete and team. It is the glue that holds everything together. Competitors that lack it find their goals much harder to achieve.

"Trust your teammates" is a phrase that I repeat to the athletes that I coach. Too often an athlete will try to take on too much responsibility and try to make plays that are not wise or are beyond their ability. This usually happens when they do not trust that their teammates will be able to make the play.

People will be inspired to raise their level of production when others place confidence in them.

Trust is an amazing thing. People will be inspired to raise their level of production when others place confidence in them. I have seen athletes step up and make plays that they weren't used to making simply because their teammates trusted them and gave them the opportunity to contribute. On the flip side, I have seen athletes become discouraged and perform poorly when they are not trusted.

Players, trust your coach—or if you are a coach, trust your athletes. There is nothing goofier than to watch a coach and players who are not on the same page. The coach is in place to provide leadership so that the team will reach their potential. He or she is the focal point for training and strategy. When players undermine the leader by choosing to compete differently from the way they are coached, it causes dysfunction and destroys team unity. Parents many times will also create problems by telling their child to do things differently than the way the coach is instructing them.

I know this will sound strange at first glance, but think about it for a minute. Even if the coach is wrong in their strategy, it is still harmful to buck his or her system. If an athlete or parent is really in strong disagreement with a coach's approach, he or she should seriously consider leaving the team and finding a place that is a better fit.

If a coach's training involves being abusive or endangering an athlete's well being, that is a different story. That situation should be addressed directly with the appropriate people.

Finally, in addition to trusting your teammates or coaches, trust yourself. Sports have lots of ups and downs. It's easy to be confident when things are going well but much more difficult when times are tough. One of the mental challenges that an athlete faces is to have confidence when there is no reason to. Success begins with a belief in yourself. When that is absent, the task will seem insurmountable.

Trust those around you. It will make the journey much smoother.

Playbook Perspective

A troublemaker plants seeds of strife; gossip separates the best of friends.
Proverbs 16:28

Questions for Reflection and Discussion

Athletes
- Do you trust what your coach tells you?
- Do you trust your teammates to make plays?
- Do you trust yourself to make plays?

Coaches
- Do your athletes feel like you have confidence in them?
- Have you taught them to trust one another?
- Have you taught them to have confidence in themselves?

Parents
- Does your child feel like you believe in him or her?
- Does your coach feel like you believe in him or her?

32

Actions Lead Better Than Words

Some years ago a trio of freshmen guys came to play basketball at the University of Toledo. Each arrived with high hopes of a great college basketball career and the desire to play at the next level beyond college. However, after they arrived at UT, the reality of their new environment set in and the hard work began.

The trio's freshman year wasn't quite the glamour and glory that they had envisioned. However, this was a special group of guys who had a burning desire to achieve their potential and be the very best team they could be.

Justin Ingram, Keonta Howell, and Tino Valencia developed their skills. Self-discipline, confidence, good decision-making, and consistency were things that had to be learned in order to achieve their goal. They realized that talking about a conference championship would not make it happen. They actually needed to put in the time to make it a reality. Justin, Keonta, and Tino were often in the gym shooting, dribbling, and running on their own. Even when no one else was looking, they were committed to their goal.

Their senior year arrived in Fall 2006 and it had been twenty-five years since Toledo had won a Mid-American Conference basketball championship. Hopes were high. Tragically, during the preseason, post player, Haris Charalambous, collapsed and passed away on the school track during conditioning. The team was devastated.

The team pulled together and started their quest. The preconference schedule was tough but prepared them for the challenge when conference play began. As the season wore on, these three seniors were able to lead the team to a 16–2 conference record and secure UT's first regular season conference championship in twenty-five years.

> ***They realized that talking about their goal wasn't good enough. In order to own their dream, they needed to take action.***

The hard work that Justin, Keonta, and Tino put in outside of normal practice helped them to achieve their goal. They realized that talking about their goal wasn't good enough. In order to own their dream, they needed to take action. Incidentally, all three guys went on to play professionally overseas.

Take a page from Justin, Keonta, and Tino's playbook. Let your actions lead more than your words.

Playbook Perspective

> *Lazy people want much but get little, but those who work hard will prosper.*
> *Proverbs 13:4*

Questions for Reflection and Discussion

Athletes
- Are you a talker or a doer?
- Do you lead your team with your actions?
- What actions do you need to take in order to lead better?

Coaches
- Are your actions consistent with your words?
- Do you practice and model the principles that you teach to your athletes?
- How do you motivate your athletes to lead by his or her actions?

Parents
- Are your actions consistent with your words?
- Do you encourage your child to lead with his or her actions?

33

Play the Right Way

In sports, as well as in the real world, everyone wants to get an edge on the competition by finding opportunities to tip the scales in his or her direction. Sometimes, the lines between what is or isn't acceptable get quite blurry. Given the right motivation, it can be easy to make small compromises, which have the potential to lead to bigger compromises.

As a coach, I have been tempted to bend the rules in order to win. However, I always quickly realize the foolishness of that temptation. Even if I was the only one that knew, I would always hate to have anything taint my accomplishments. In my opinion, there is nothing worse than to achieve my goals using an underhanded approach and wonder if I really could have pulled it off doing things the right way.

There are some people who only care about the final score and the end result.

I suppose not everyone sees things that way and it's a shame. There are some people who only care about the final score and the end result. Over the years, I've tried to steer clear of this pitfall by adhering to one of my core values: I believe that how we play is just as important as the outcome of the contest. Therefore, I constantly tell my teams, "Play the right way, no matter what."

It doesn't matter what your opponent has done, you should be committed to play according to the rules of the game. Just because an opponent gets away with something illegal doesn't give you the right to play that way. The key to playing the right way is to focus on your goals, objectives, and game plan rather than on how your opponent is trying to distract you.

Another aspect of playing the right way is to not take shortcuts in training. There is always a temptation to not be fundamentally sound when training times are more relaxed. However, athletes will generally compete in the same way that they practice.

Be careful to avoid the trap of compromise. It will only steal joy and satisfaction from your accomplishments.

Play the right way!

Playbook Perspective

A wise person chooses the right road; a fool takes the wrong one.
Ecclesiastes 10:2

Questions for Reflection and Discussion

Athletes

- Do you ever try to break the rules out of frustration or to get an advantage?
- Do you ever take shortcuts in training?

Coaches

- Do you always tell your team to compete according to the rules regardless of what the other team is doing?
- Do you ever take shortcuts in your preparation or training of your team?

Parents

- Do you ever encourage your child to get back at an opponent?
- Do you try to put your child on teams that have coaches who are committed to doing things the right way?

34

Make Your Teammates Better

Erica was one of the smallest girls on her youth soccer team. At first glance, one would think that she was too little to play the game. As I began to coach her, I found out quickly that she was one of the toughest competitors that I had ever coached. After I watched Erica bounce back from several big collisions that would have left most other girls flat on their backs, I began to believe that she was truly indestructible.

Nothing would keep Erica away from soccer. She loved it! Her work ethic to develop her skills and her sheer determination made her a leader on the team. Yet, there was something else that set her apart and made her a special player: Erica's desire to help her teammates succeed.

Athletes who listen, tirelessly execute, and exhibit humility help make their team better every day.

Erica always looked for every opportunity to set her teammates up for success. To her, an assist was just as good as a goal. Rather than just trying to build her own statistics, Erica would involve her teammates in the flow of the game, which built their confidence and made them better.

In a close game, I could always count on Erica to raise her level of intensity. On several occasions, her increased hustle created opportunities to score and inspired her teammates to raise their level of play.

In a day and age when many athletes are looking out for their own glory, it is refreshing for a coach to work with athletes who desire the best for their team. Athletes who listen, tirelessly execute, and exhibit humility help make their team better every day.

Finding fulfillment in your sport should come mostly in celebrating the team accomplishments. Individual recognition may come, but it should not be the primary goal. Instead, do whatever is necessary to inspire your teammates and make them better.

Playbook Perspective

A person standing alone can be attacked and defeated, but two can stand back-to-back and conquer. Three are even better, for a triple-braided cord is not easily broken. Ecclesiastes 4:12

Questions for Reflection and Discussion

Athletes

- Are you more concerned about your statistics than about how the team performs?
- Do you help your teammates maximize their strengths?
- Will you help a teammate improve even if it means he or she might take your spot?

Coaches

- Do you promote a team concept or do you value individual performance?
- Do you show athletes how they can help make their teammates better?

Parents

- Are you more concerned about your child's performance or about the team's performance?
- Do you encourage your child to invest in his or her teammates?

35

Performance Does Not Define Me

As Wendy and I work with college athletes year after year, a common issue rises to the surface more than any other: Their sport becomes their identity. Because college athletes have spent a tremendous amount of time working for the opportunity to compete in their sport at this level, they are easily caught up in this snare.

In the midst of reaching this apex, a new reality comes into play. No longer are they dominant in competition like they were in high school. College draws the top athletes from high school and competition is much fiercer, not only when competing against other schools but among their teammates as well.

Athletes who reach the college level have gotten there by pouring their lives into their sport and have found great satisfaction along the way. Unexpectedly they find that the sport has become the most important thing in their lives. Their performance becomes the indicator for how well their lives are going. If they perform well, they feel good about themselves and their lives. If they perform poorly, they feel lousy about themselves and their lives. Injuries complicate that even more.

> *At higher levels of competition it becomes progressively more difficult to separate the sport (what you do) from who you are.*

At higher levels of competition it becomes progressively more difficult to separate the sport (what you do) from who you are. This same pattern, if not identified and corrected, will carry past graduation into the working world where your job will define you in the same way that your sport did. Not only does this affect athletes but coaches as well.

In order to keep this reality from taking place, the athlete or coach needs to create boundaries and maintain mental discipline to not allow sport to take a place that it was never designed to have. As a coach, I am constantly tempted to let my team's performance define my value as a coach and as a person.

When I allow that temptation to take root, it damages my relationships with the most important people in my life because a poor team performance will put me in a bad mood for the rest of the day and maybe into the next. Does that mean that I should be happy about a poor performance? Absolutely not. I need to learn from it and turn the negative performance into a positive moment that moves me toward future success.

But think about it. Does being in a bad mood make a poor performance any better? No. Am I a worse coach because we had a poor performance? No. Should I take a bad performance out on my family and friends? No, they don't deserve that. I am the same person whether I or my team performs well or performs poorly.

When a sport takes the center place in our lives, dysfunction occurs and we suffer the consequences. I also believe that when this dysfunction occurs, it introduces factors that hinder performance on the field of competition as well. Do yourself a favor and put boundaries on your sport so that it doesn't control your life and emotions. Make a commitment to yourself that "PERFORMANCE DOES NOT DEFINE ME."

Playbook Perspective

> *You made all the delicate, inner parts of my body and knit me together in my mother's womb. Thank you for making me so wonderfully complex! Your workmanship is marvelous—how well I know it.*
> *Psalm 139:13-14*

Questions for Reflection and Discussion

Athletes

- Does the way you are performing determine how you feel about yourself?
- Do you find value in yourself outside of your sport?
- Is your sport ruling your life?

Coaches

- Do you communicate how you value an athlete based on how he or she performs?
- Do you find your own value in how your team performs?
- How can you put boundaries around how your coaching influences the rest of your life?

Parents

- Does your child find his/her value as a person by how he or she performs in his or her sport?
- How can you help your child see his or her true value as a person and not allow the sport to control his or her life?

36

Know Yourself

One of the most important things that athletes can do is to realistically assess their strengths and weaknesses. No athlete is excellent in every skill in their sport, even those who play at the professional level. For players to achieve their potential, they must learn how to maximize their strengths and minimize their weaknesses.

Many young athletes will watch a professional athlete use particular skills and then try to imitate those same skills in competition. The youngsters obviously are unable to perform those skills, but that doesn't stop them from hoping that something magical will happen in the moment. Mature athletes would never use skills they have not mastered in a competitive situation. Instead, they discipline themselves to compete utilizing the abilities that best give them the opportunity for success.

As a soccer player, it was important for me to recognize I could significantly change through hard work and to identify what would be difficult, if not impossible, to change no matter the amount of time or effort that I invested. Although I had decent

Over time, I figured out where my gifts and abilities were best utilized on the soccer field, which allowed me to enjoy a satisfying athletic career.

speed, I was not going to blaze past other players on the field. However, I could greatly improve my hand and feet dexterity by working on ball skills regularly.

Over time, I figured out where my gifts and abilities were best utilized on the soccer field, which allowed me to enjoy a satisfying athletic career. As a coach, I have to recognize my strengths and weaknesses that impact my leadership. I realized early on that I needed to bring people around me who have strengths that were different from mine. One lesson I realized is that if I try to fake my way through my weaknesses, they become even more glaring.

Don't try to be someone you are not. Rather, celebrate your gifts and abilities. Work hard to strengthen those gifts so that you can achieve your God-given potential. Get honest feedback and input from others who know you well and can give you an objective assessment.

Know yourself.

Playbook Perspective

Wise words bring many benefits, and hard work brings rewards. Fools think their own way is right, but the wise listen to others.
Proverbs 12:14-15

Questions for Reflection and Discussion

Athletes

- What are your strengths as an athlete?
- What are your weaknesses as an athlete?
- How can you maximize your strengths and minimize your weaknesses?

Coaches

- How well do you know your athletes' strengths and weaknesses?
- How well do you know your own strengths and weaknesses?
- Are you able to maximize the strengths and minimize the weaknesses on your team?

Parents

- How well do you know your child's strengths and weaknesses?
- Are you able to help your child maximize his or her strengths and minimize his or her weaknesses?

37

Don't Hold Back

Constant energy was the trademark of Johnnie LaPrairie. He played midfield on a high school boys soccer team that I coached about twenty-five years ago. I loved to watch him play because there was never any doubt that I was getting his best effort every time he entered the field of play. Whether he was dribbling the ball or chasing down an attacker, Johnnie had one speed—full throttle, and his teammates fed off that intense energy. I can still picture his determined face and his arms pumping continuously as he motored down the field.

When we hold back from giving our best effort, we create regrets and live with excuses.

As a coach, I have always loved having players like Johnnie. In contrast, I have coached athletes who held back for one reason or another. Some were concerned about getting injured, whereas others just hadn't pushed themselves hard enough. Then there was the category of players that simply did not care about being the best they could be. When we hold back from giving our best effort, we create regrets and live with excuses. "If I would have …" "I just let them…" "If only…"

Sometimes athletes refrain from giving their best effort due to fear of injury. However, it has been my experience that the athletes who hold back are just as much at risk for injury as those who compete without fear. Many times a player trying to avoid injury ends up with an injury. Holding back doesn't necessarily help someone to stay out of harm's way.

Not understanding what it means to compete is another big reason that athletes give less than their best. They simply haven't pushed themselves to their potential. They think they are competing hard, but there is a whole new level they can reach if they choose to push past the mental barriers that cap their development.

There is great satisfaction in pushing through the hurdles that threaten to stagnate our growth and limit our potential. Don't hold back. You will find personal treasure by giving your best effort and overcoming the roadblocks in your path.

Playbook Perspective

Work brings profit, but mere talk leads to poverty!
Proverbs 14:23

Questions for Reflection and Discussion

Athletes

- What keeps you from giving your best effort?
- Do you make a lot of excuses for your performance or lack of effort?
- What would it take for you to overcome your mental blocks and give your best effort every time you compete?

Coaches

- What keeps your athletes from giving their best effort?
- How are you able to motivate them past their mental blocks?
- What are the mental blocks that you need to overcome as a coach?

Parents

- What mental blocks keep your child from giving his or her best effort?
- How will you help him or her to overcome those areas?

38

Everyone Needs a Sunday

While I played soccer in college, I also held a job one fall loading semi trucks at UPS. My job was Monday through Friday 4 a.m. to 8 a.m. I would have class 8 a.m. to 12 p.m. and practice 3 p.m. to 6 p.m. when we weren't playing games. For several weeks during that stretch I would sleep only three to four hours per night.

It was a pretty intense time keeping up with my studies, work, and soccer. It became so demanding that I came really close to quitting the team, but I ended up sticking it out. However, I began to have a number of injuries. No surprise, though. Limited sleep combined with demanding physical training meant there was insufficient recovery time for my body. It took time for me to learn that adequate rest is an essential part of success in sports.

Sometimes, however, we find out too late that too much of a good thing is not always helpful.

When we want to get better at something, we figure out ways to invest more time and energy into it. That is true of sports as well. We find ways to improve our conditioning and skill training. We schedule more competitions. We do this to maximize our athletic potential.

Sometimes, however, we find out too late that too much of a good thing is not always helpful. As I have worked with athletes of all ages, I have found that it is becoming more common for athletes to overwork their bodies. I see more boots (particularly on girls) to provide relief from stress fractures. As a disclaimer, I am not a medical professional but I have been around sports long enough to observe what overworked bodies experience.

Most athletes don't experience such intensity that their bodies shut down that quickly. However, over time, the constant pounding from training can take its toll. I've experienced this with my kids. There have been times when we have had to eliminate or severely limit training for several months in order to allow their bodies to recover.

I'm convinced that every athlete needs at least one day each week away from training to allow themselves the time to be refreshed both mentally and physically. Hence, after years of crazy sports schedules, we've decided that sports will not be more than six days a week. We often choose Sundays as our day away. Only on occasions do we go to a Sunday sports event.

In addition to the physical and mental benefits of a day off, it gives our family a chance to connect relationally and slow our life pace a little. With having had five kids involved in multiple sports, this is valuable as a family.

Try it. You might really like it. Everyone needs a Sunday.

Playbook Perspective

For in six days the Lord made heaven and earth, but on the seventh day he stopped working and was refreshed.
Exodus 31:17

Questions for Reflection and Discussion

Athletes

- Does your body get enough rest to recover from competitions?
- Do you have frequent injuries?
- Do you have enough breaks in your schedule to refresh yourself mentally and spiritually?

Coaches

- Do you give your athletes enough recovery time so that their bodies are able to perform at optimal levels?
- Do your athletes have enough down time to refresh their minds and spirits?
- Do you have enough down time to stay sharp physically, mentally, and spiritually?

Parents

- Does your child experience anxiety due to his or her schedule?
- Does your child experience frequent injuries that might be related to overload?
- What adjustments can you make to help your child?

39

Facing the Giants

One of the toughest challenges in sports is competing against an opponent who you know is much better than you. No one likes to be embarrassed and thrashed in a competition by a superior opponent—we'll call that kind of an opponent "the Giant."

Often less superior athletes approach these "David vs. Goliath" situations with two different mind-sets. One mind-set realizes the substantial gap between the two competitors and simply hopes to make a good showing, while not being completely overwhelmed. The other common mind-set takes an overly optimistic view, believing that they will triumph over their giant, mainly because they "want it more."

There is a self-confidence, that despite the odds, they can overcome the giant they are facing.

Neither of those mind-sets works very well. However, it is possible to strike a good balance. Every so often the underdog pulls off the big upset, and one of the reasons they do is because they approach the competitive event with the right mind-set.

Underdogs that are able to knock off the giant can do so because they start with a healthy respect for their opponent. They know what the opposition is capable of but they also understand where they are vulnerable. They have a realistic view of the situation and enter with a locked-in focus.

Secondly, underdogs are not in awe of the opposition. They understand that their opponent needs to earn the victory. There is a self-confidence that despite the odds, they can overcome the giant they are facing.

Strong competitors can sense a lack of confidence in their underdog opponents—and they will exploit it to their advantage. While a lack of confidence can demoralize a competitor sending them to defeat, overconfidence will do the same. Overconfidence will deflate at the first sign of trouble and everything will unravel from there. It is important to maintain a healthy sense of confidence without getting cocky.

When you face the giants, attack with a good game plan and stay confident regardless of the score. Who knows, you just might pull off something really big.

Playbook Perspective

We even saw giants there, the descendants of Anak. Next to them we felt like grasshoppers, and that's what they thought, too.
Numbers 13:33

Questions for Reflection and Discussion

Athletes

- Have you ever faced an overwhelming challenge? How did you respond?
- Do you anticipate big challenges or do you dread them?
- How will you prepare for your next giant?

Coaches

- How do you prepare your team to face the giant?
- How do you personally prepare to coach against the giant?

Parents

- How does your child handle giants in his or her life?
- How do you help your child prepare to meet the giants in his or her life?

40

Don't Underestimate Your Opponent

Everyone was jawing it up about by how many points they would win the game. My seventh grade son, Josh, was travelling with his basketball team to play a team for the second time during the season. In their previous game, Josh's team blew out their opponent by thirty points.

When an individual or a team doesn't give proper respect to an opponent, they put themselves at risk to perform poorly.

The boys had a rude awakening as they found themselves down by six points after the first quarter. The rest of the game was a battle! While Josh's team won by three points, underestimating their opponent almost cost the boys the victory.

The best competitor does not always win. You can observe this at every level of sports. When an individual or a team doesn't give proper respect to an opponent, they put themselves at risk to perform poorly. Often a team's loss can be traced back to a lapse in mental preparation because they didn't fully respect their competitor.

When you compete, make sure that you mentally prepare for every opponent as if you were competing in a championship that day. Don't underestimate your opponent because it will probably come back to haunt you if you do.

Playbook Perspective

> *Or suppose a king is about to go to war against another king. Will he not first sit down and consider whether he is able with ten thousand men to oppose the one coming with twenty thousand?*
> Luke 14:31 NIV

Questions for Reflection and Discussion

Athletes

- Can you remember a time when you underestimated your opponent? How did it affect your performance?
- How can you adjust your mental preparation when you are facing a weaker opponent?

Coaches

- How do you prepare for facing a weaker opponent?
- How can you help your team avoid underestimating an opponent?

Parents

- How do you help your child avoid being overconfident for an upcoming competition?
- Have you ever helped fuel your child to be overconfident? How did it affect their performance?

"There is life beyond soccer," said Coach Matt. My teammates and I were huddled together sitting Indian style in a circle. We have sat like this many times going over different words that we could apply to soccer and life. We learned powerful words like *tenacity, teamwork, focusing,* and *determination.* My coach, Matt Yeager, spewed out new words each week that we would use during practice. Here is a man who could teach life lessons through the amazing sport called soccer. Who knew that soccer and life were so closely related? Come to think of it, everything I need to know came from him. The following principles that he taught me will last forever, and I can't thank him enough for teaching them to me. Coach Matt taught me teamwork and humility, life beyond soccer, and that I may not always win everything that I attempt.

My coach taught me about teamwork and humility through various means. Being a team was very important to him. For instance, I remember a few players misbehaving during practice; instead of just punishing those players, he reprimanded us all. The whole team ended up running because he wanted us to realize that any mistakes one player may make will eventually affect the entire team. Another way Coach Yeager taught me teamwork and humility was through his actions. He tried very hard to make playing time equal, and he told us that there were no superstars on the team. His principles about acting like a team and not as an individual were necessary lessons to learn.

Next, my coach told us, "There is more to life than soccer." This was a valuable lesson that I needed to learn. First, he taught us this by discussing topics, such as personal excellence, that I could not only apply to soccer but to life. Also, he supported me and other players doing activities outside of soccer. He allowed me to sometimes miss practice when I had other commitments. Because we were so young, our coach wanted us to know that we should be experiencing all the different avenues in life.

Finally, Matt Yeager didn't forget to teach me that it is impossible to win everything.

After each loss, he told us to "nail it and press on" (put it behind you). Then, we went over our mistakes and fixed them. I also learned this concept from how he acted after a huge defeat. After receiving second place twice to the same team, he told us how proud he was despite our not coming in first. By not pressuring us to be the very best, I learned a great deal about winning and losing.

So, why is humility and teamwork, life beyond sports, and understanding that you can't win all the time important? Inevitably, I will have to deal with these issues at different times throughout my existence. Therefore, I should be better prepared for certain circumstances all because of one fantastic soccer coach. "Hey coach, did I get it right?"

Written by Bethany Brown

Personal Commitment

The following contains a loose summary of many of the concepts incorporated in this book. It is intended for you to post these as a reminder of the principles discussed in this book. They also will be available for download at our website true-sport.org.

Personal Commitment for the Athlete

I make this promise to myself to:

• Compete every day as if it is my last chance to do so and pursue excellence.

• Not live in the past but look forward to make the next play.

• Not cheat myself or my teammates but compete with relentless dedication.

• Never, never, never give up.

• Respect my coaches, opponents, and officials even when I think they're wrong.

• Stay positive and learn from difficult circumstances and criticism.

• Overcome fear by facing it with confidence.

• Be humble when success arrives.

• Do things the right way and take responsibility for my actions.

• Be a team player and trust those around me.

• Make wise sacrifices.

• Believe in my value as a person and not base that value on my performance.

Personal Commitment for the Coach

I make this promise to myself to:

• Be patient with the development of my team.

• Communicate with honor and respect to my athletes, parents, and officials.

• Recognize the deep impact my words and actions have on my team.

• Elevate my frustration to become a better coach.

• Be humble when success arrives.

• Maintain discipline, but do it with a positive tone.

• Recognize that in the end it's just a game.

• Encourage my team to compete within the spirit and letter of the rules.

• Facilitate time away from the sport for my athletes to be refreshed.

• Never, never, never give up on my team or any individual.

• Respond with grace when criticism and hardship arrive.

Personal Commitment for the Parent

I make this promise to myself to:

• Help encourage my child to relentless dedication of their sport.

• Not hold unrealistic expectations of my child, his or her coach, and team results.

• Find positive things to encourage my child.

• Not allow my own sense of worth to be tied to my child's performance.

• Communicate respectfully with officials, coaches, and my child.

• Help my child to develop character in difficult circumstances.

• Not allow sports to force sacrifice of more important things.

• Encourage my child to pursue excellence.

• Ensure that my child has enough "down time" in his or life.

• Be humble when my child has success.

• Elevate my frustration when watching my child compete.